COMPLETE BOOK
of First Grade

The sun is bright!

Thinking Kids®
An imprint of Carson Dellosa Education
Greensboro, NC

Thinking Kids®
Carson Dellosa Education
PO Box 35665
Greensboro, NC 27425 USA

ISBN 978-1-4838-6238-5

01-067211151

Dear Parents, Caregivers, and Educators,

The *Complete Book* series provides young learners an exciting and dynamic way to learn the basic skills essential to learning success. This vivid workbook will guide your student step-by-step through a variety of engaging and developmentally appropriate activities in basic concepts, reading, math, language arts, writing, and fine motor skills.

The *Complete Book of First Grade* is designed to be used with an adult's support. Your student will gain the most when you work together through the activities. Below are a few suggestions to help make the most of your learning time together:

- Read the directions aloud. Move your finger under the words as your child watches. As you come to words he or she recognizes, encourage your student to read along.
- Explain the activities in terms your student understands. Talk about the pictures and activities. These conversations will both strengthen your student's confidence and build important language skills.
- Provide support and encouragement to your student. Work with your student at a pace that is comfortable for him or her. End your learning time when your student shows signs of tiring.

To find other learning materials that will interest your young learner and encourage school success, visit www.carsondellosa.com

TABLE OF CONTENTS

Letter Detective: Ii

Directions: Say the name of each picture. If it has a short i sound, color it yellow. If it has a long i sound, color it red.

ĭ

ī

Name _____

Letter Detective: Oo

Directions: The short **o** sounds like the **o** in **dog**. Long **o** sounds like the **o** in **rope**. Draw a line from the picture to the word that names it. Draw a circle around the word if it has a short **o** sound.

hot dog

fox

blocks

rose

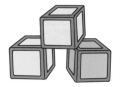

boat

Letter Detective: Oo

Directions: Say the name of each picture. If the picture has the long **o** sound, write a **green** L on the blank. If the picture has the short **o** sound, write a **red** S on the blank.

Letter Detective: Uu

Directions: The short **u** sounds like the **u** in **bug**. The long **u** sounds like the **u** in **blue**. Draw a circle around the words with short **u**. Draw an **X** on the words with long **u**.

rug   cup   music

tub   suit   glue

bug   puppy   gum

Letter Detective: Uu

Directions: Say the name of each picture. If it has the short **u** sound, write a **u** in the **umbrella** column. If it has the long **u** sound, write a **u** in the **unicorn** column.

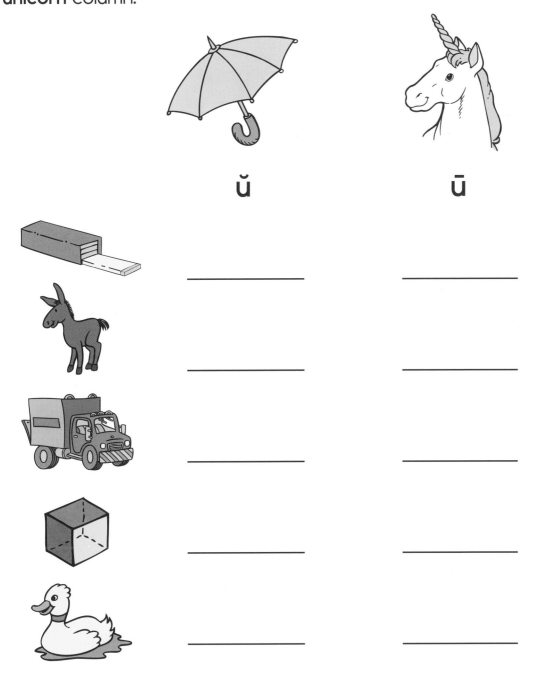

ŭ   ū

_____   _____

_____   _____

_____   _____

_____   _____

_____   _____

Name _____

Super Silent E

When you add an **e** to the end of some words, the vowel changes from a short vowel sound to a long vowel sound. The **e** is silent.

Example: rip + **e** = ripe

Directions: Say the word under the first picture in each pair. Then, add an **e** to the word under the next picture. Say the new word.

pet   _____   tub   _____

man   _____   kit   _____

pin   _____   cap   _____

My Vowel List

Keep this list handy and add more words to it.

short a
(ă as in cat)
_____

long a
(ā as in train)
_____

short e
(ĕ as in get)
_____

long e
(ē as in tree)
_____

short i
(ĭ as in pin)
_____

long i
(ī as in ice)
_____

short o
(ŏ as in cot)
_____

long o
(ō as in boat)
_____

short u
(ŭ as in cut)
_____

long u
(ū as in cube)
_____

This page is blank for the activity
on the opposite side.

Rhythm and Rhyme

Rhyming words are words that sound alike at the end of the word.

Directions: Draw a line to match the pictures that rhyme. Write two of your rhyming word pairs below.

_____   _____

_____   _____

_____   _____

_____   _____

Name _____

A, B, C Dinosaur

Directions: Abc order is the order in which letters come in the alphabet. Draw a line to connect the dots. Follow the letters in **abc** order. Then, color the picture.

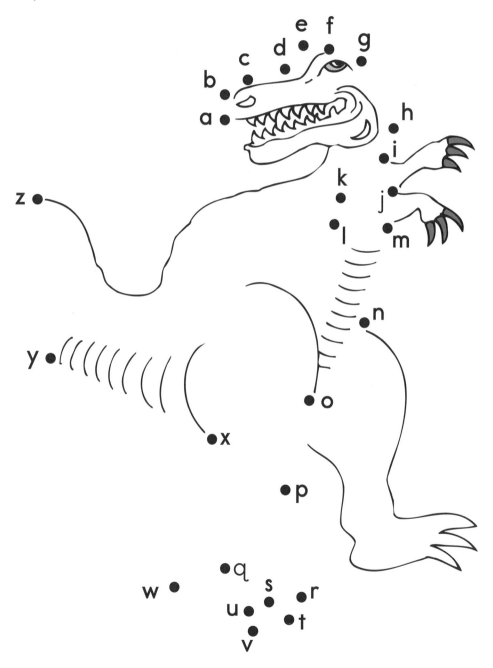

Putting Things in Order

Directions: Circle the first letter of each word. Then, put each pair of words in **abc** order.

(C)ar   (b)ird   moon   two

bird

car

nest   fan   card   dog

pig   bike   sun   pie

Two Words in One

Compound words are two words that are put together to make one new word.

Directions: Look at the pictures and the two words that are next to each other. Put the words together to make a new word. Write the new word.

Example:

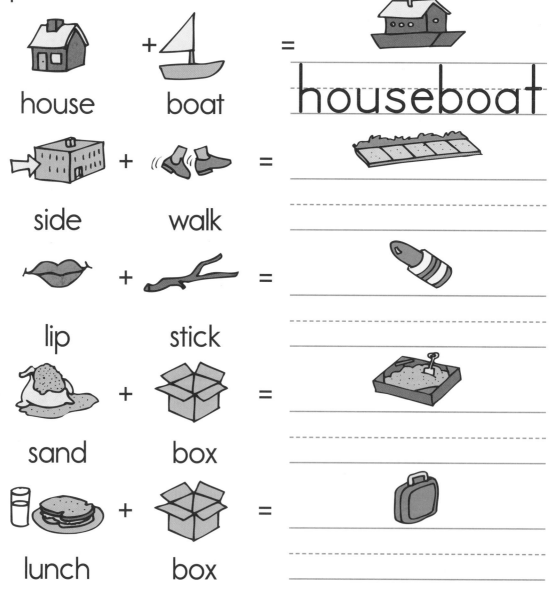

house + boat = houseboat

side + walk = _____

lip + stick = _____

sand + box = _____

lunch + box = _____

Double the Fun

Directions: Cut out the cards below. Turn them over. Take turns trying to make compound words. When a compound word is made, the player gets to keep the word.

Cut ✂ --

flash	snow	ball	sun
mail	house	plant	room
light	bow	light	card
base	shine	dog	box
rain	flake	thing	post
family	house	in	house
any	side	day	birth

This page is blank for the cutting activity
on the opposite side.

The Name Game

You are a special person. Your name begins with a capital letter. We put a capital letter at the beginning of people's names because they are special.

Directions: Write your name. Did you remember to use a capital letter?

_____

- -

_____

Directions: Write each person's name. Use a capital letter at the beginning.

Ted _____

Katie _____

Marcos _____

Tim _____

Write a friend's name. Use a capital letter at the beginning.

_____

7 Delightful Days

The days of the week begin with capital letters.

Directions: Write the days of the week in the spaces below. Put them in order. Be sure to start with capital letters.

Tuesday
_____

Saturday
_____

Monday
_____

Friday
_____

Thursday
_____

Sunday
_____

Wednesday
_____

12 Marvelous Months

he months of the year begin with capital letters.

Directions: Write the months of the year in order on the calendar below. e sure to use capital letters.

| January | July | June | April | November | February |
| October | December | March | September | May | August |

_____   _____

_____   _____

_____   _____

_____   _____

_____   _____

_____   _____

Name _____

Little Riddles

Directions: Read the word and write it on the line. Then, read each riddle and draw a line to the picture and word that tells about it.

house

_____

_____

I like to play.
I am little. I am soft.
What am I?

kitten

_____

_____

I am big.
People live in me.
What am I?

flower

_____

_____

I am pretty.
I am green and yellow.
What am I?

pony

_____

_____

I can jump. I can run.
I am brown
What am I?

Get the Picture?

Directions: Read the sentence. Circle the word that makes sense. Use the picture clues to help you. Then, write the word.

I ride on a _____.

bike   hike

I ride on a _____.

train   tree

I ride in a _____.

car   can

I ride on a _____.

bus   bug

I ride in a _____.

jar   jet

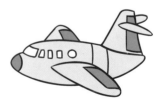

I ride in a _____.

took   truck

Winter Warmers

Directions: Color the things that keep you warm.

socks

earmuffs

apple

lunch box

hat

coat

umbrella

cookie

gloves

Sunlight, Moonlight

Directions: Write the words from the box under the pictures they describe.

stars	sun	moon	rays
dark	light	night	day

Like It or Not

Directions: Circle the picture in each row that is most like the first picture.

Example:

carrot   jacks   bread   pea

baseball   sneakers   basketball   bat

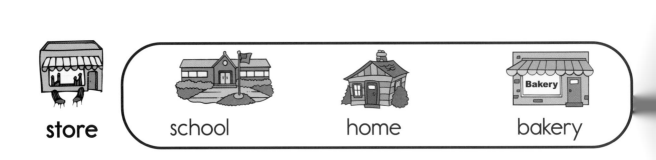

store   school   home   bakery

kitten   dog   fox   cat

Odd One Out

Directions: Draw an **X** on the picture that does not belong in each group.

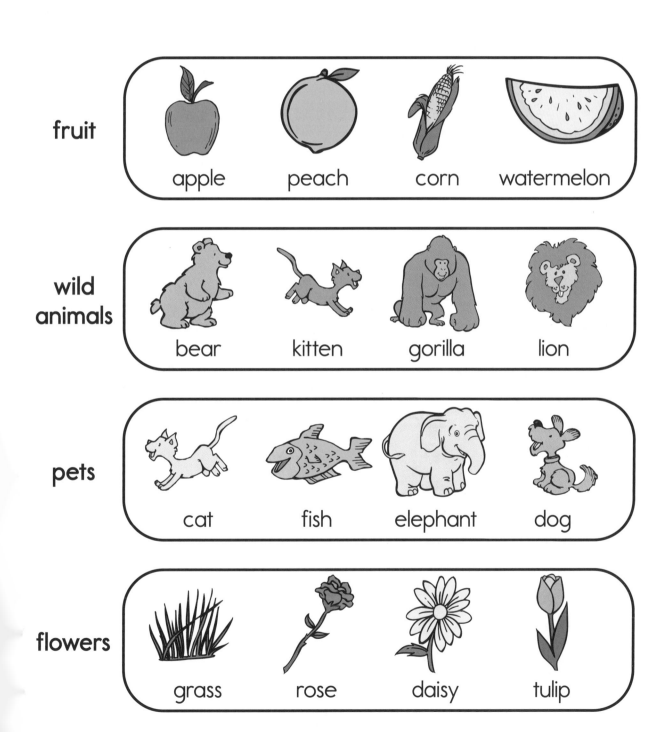

fruit — apple · peach · corn · watermelon

wild animals — bear · kitten · gorilla · lion

pets — cat · fish · elephant · dog

flowers — grass · rose · daisy · tulip

Name _____

See It, Sort It

Directions: Write each word in the correct row at the bottom of the page.

airplane   plate   car

pencil   spoon   crayon

chalk   fork   boat

Things we ride in:

_____

- -

_____

Things we eat with:

_____

- -

_____

Things we draw with:

_____

- -

_____

Time to Rhyme

Directions: Circle the pictures in each row that rhyme.

Row 1

Row 2

Row 3

Directions: Write the names of the pictures that do not rhyme.

These words do not rhyme:

Row 1	Row 2	Row 3
_____	_____	_____

Name _____

Twice the Fun!

Directions: Read the story. Then, use the words in the box and the picture to write your answers.

Ben and Ann are twin babies. They were born at the same time. They have the same mother. Ben is a boy baby. Ann is a girl baby.

mother	girl
bow	hat
boy	twins

1. Tell one way Ann and Ben are the same.

   _____

   _____

   _____

   _____

   _____

2. Ann and Ben are _____.

3. Tell two ways Ann and Ben are different.

   _____   _____

   Ann is a _____. Ben is a _____

   _____

   Ann is wearing a _____.

   _____

   Ben is wearing a _____.

Map It!

Directions: Color the path the girl should take to go home. Use the sentences to help you.

1. Go to the school and turn left.

2. At the end of the street, turn right.

3. Walk past the park and turn right.

4. After you pass the pool, turn right.

Make a Snowman!

Directions: Write the number of the sentence that goes with each picture in the circle.

1. Roll a large snowball for the snowman's bottom.

2. Make another snowball and put it on top of the first.

3. Put the last snowball on top.

4. Dress the snowman.

How Does Your Garden Grow?

Directions: Read the story. Then, write the steps to grow a flower.

First find a sunny spot. Then, plant the seed. Water it. The flower will start to grow. Pull the weeds around it. Remember to keep giving the flower water. Enjoy your flower.

1. _____

2. _____

3. _____

4. _____

5. _____

On the Pond

Directions: Look at the picture. Write the words from the box to finish the sentences.

> frog   log   bird   fish   ducks

_____

The _____ can jump.

The turtle is on a _____.

A _____ is in the tree.

The boy wants a _____.

I see three _____.

Name _____

An Apple a Day

Directions: Read about apples. Then, write the answers.

I like . Do you?

Some are red.

Some are green.

Some are yellow.

1. How many kinds of apples does the story tell about?

   _____

   -

   _____

2. Name the kinds of apples.

   _____   _____   _____

   - - - - - - - - -   - - - - - - - - -   - - - - - - - - -

   _____   _____   _____

3. What kind of apple do you like best?

   _____

   -

   _____

Puddle Jumping

Directions: Read the story. Write the words from the story that complete each sentence.

Jada and Bill like to play in the rain. They take off their shoes and socks. They splash in the puddles. It feels cold! It is fun to splash!

_____

Jada and Bill like to _____.

_____

They take off their _____.

_____

They splash in _____.

Do you like to splash in puddles?   Yes   No

Falling Leaves

Directions: Read about raking leaves. Then, answer the questions.

I like to rake leaves. Do you? Leaves die each year. They get brown and dry. They fall from the trees. Then, we rake them up.

1. What color are leaves when they die?

   _____

   -

   _____

2. What happens when they die?

   _____

   -

   _____

   -

   _____

3. What do we do when leaves fall?

   _____

   -

   _____

Bunches of Balloons

Directions: Read the story. Then, answer the questions.

Some balloons float. They are filled with gas. Some do not float. They are filled with air. Some clowns carry balloons. Balloons come in many colors. What color do you like?

1. What makes balloons float? _____

2. What is in balloons that do not float? _____

3. What shape are the balloons the clown is holding? _____

Name _____

READING

Time to Party!

Directions: Read about the party. Then, complete the invitation.

The party will be at Dog's house. The party will start at 1:00 P.M. It will last 2 hours. Write your birthday for the date of the party.

Party Invitation

Where: _____

Date: _____

Time It Begins: _____

Time It Ends: _____

_____

Directions: On the last line, write something else about the party.

Review

Directions: Read the story. Then, circle the pictures of things that are wet.

Some things used in baking are dry. Some things used in baking are wet. To bake a cake, first mix the salt, sugar and flour. Then, add the egg. Now, add the milk. Stir. Put the cake in the oven.

Directions: Tell the order to mix things when you bake a cake.

1. _____

2. _____

3. _____

4. _____

5. _____

Directions: Circle the answers.

6. The first things to mix are   dry   wet.

7. Where are cakes baked?   oven   grill

Boats Afloat

Directions: Read about boats. Then, answer the questions.

See the boats! They float on water. Some boats have sails. The wind moves the sails. It makes the boats go. Many people name their sailboats. They paint the name on the side of the boat.

1. What makes sailboats move?

   _____

   _____

   _____

2. Where do sailboats float?

   _____

   _____

   _____

3. What would you name a sailboat?

   _____

   _____

   _____

Name _____

Sail Away

Directions: Find the three boats that are alike. Color them all the same. One boat is different. Color it differently.

Gone to Sea

Directions: Write a sentence under each picture to tell what is happening. Read the story you wrote.

Name _____

What's Next?

Directions: Complete each story by choosing the correct picture. Draw a line from the story to the picture.

1. Shawnda got her books. She went to the bus stop. Shawnda got on the bus.

2. Marco planted a seed. He watered it. He pulled the weeds around it.

3. Abraham's dog was barking. Abraham got out the dog food. He put it in the dog bowl.

A Happy Ending

Directions: Read each story. Circle the sentence that tells how the story will end.

Ann was riding her bike. She saw a dog in the park. She stopped to pet it. Ann left to go home.

The dog went swimming.

The dog followed Ann.

The dog went home with a cat.

Antonio went to a baseball game. A baseball player hit a ball toward him. He reached out his hands.

The player caught the ball.

The ball bounced on a car.

Antonio caught the ball.

Name _____

How Would You Feel?

Directions: Read each story. Choose a word from the box to show how each person feels.

> happy　　excited　　sad　　mad

1. Andy and Sam were best friends. Sam and his family moved far away. How does Sam feel?

   _____

   _____

2. Deana could not sleep. It was the night before her birthday party. How does Deana feel?

   _____

   _____

3. Jacob let his baby brother play with his teddy bear. His brother lost the bear. How does Jacob feel?

   _____

   _____

4. Kia picked flowers for her mom. Her mom smiled when she got them. How does Kia feel?

   _____

   _____

English

Name ______________________________

Nouns All Around

Directions: Write these naming words in the correct box.

store	zoo	child	baby
teacher	table	cat	park
gym	woman	sock	horse

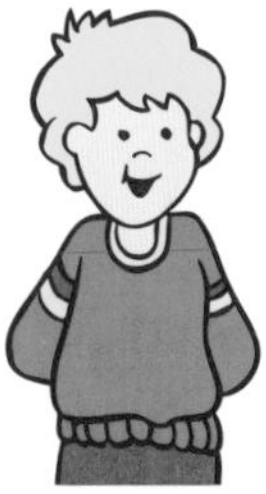

Person

______________ ______________

______________ ______________

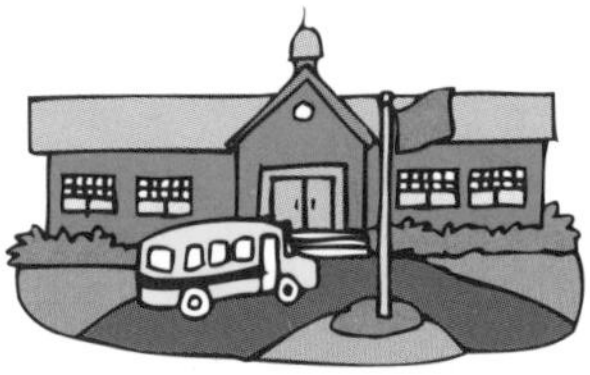

Place

______________ ______________

______________ ______________

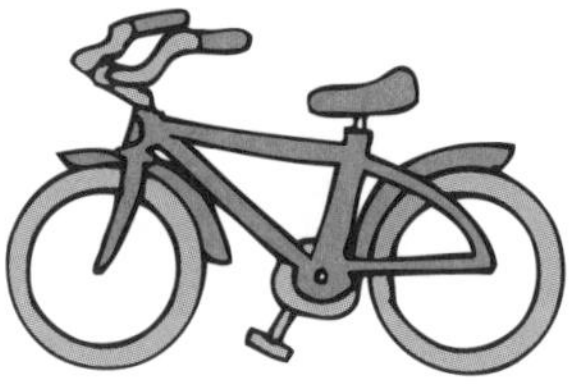

Thing

______________ ______________

______________ ______________

Pick a Pair

Some nouns name things that go together.

Directions: Draw a line to match the nouns on the left with the things they go with on the right.

toothpaste

washcloth

pencil

sock

salt

toothbrush

shoe

pepper

soap

paper

pillow

bed

Get in on the Action

Directions: Look at the picture and read the words. Write an action word in each sentence below.

swing   rings

kick

run   talk

1. The two boys like to _____ together.

2. The children _____ the soccer ball.

3. Some children like to _____ on the swing.

4. The girl can _____ very fast.

5. The teacher _____ the bell.

Review

Directions: Read the sentences below. Draw a **red** circle around the nouns. Draw a **blue** line under the verbs.

1. The boy runs fast.

2. The turtle eats leaves.

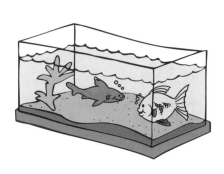

3. The fish swim in the tank.

4. The girl hits the ball.

Show and Tell

Directions: Read the words in the box. Choose the word that describes the picture. Write it next to the picture.

wet   round   funny   soft   sad   tall

1, 2, 3—Compare and See

Directions: Look at the pictures in each row. Write 1, 2 or 3 under the picture to show where it should be.

shortest _____   shorter _____   short _____

longest _____   longer _____   long _____

happy _____   happier _____   happiest _____

hotter _____   hot _____   hottest _____

Synonym Sense

Synonyms are words that mean almost the same thing. **Start** and **begin** are synonyms.

Directions: Find the synonyms that describe each picture. Write the words in the boxes next to the picture.

small	funny	large	sad
silly	little	unhappy	big

_____ _____

_____ _____

_____ _____

_____ _____

Two of a Kind

Directions: Circle the word in each row that is most like the first word in the row.

Example:

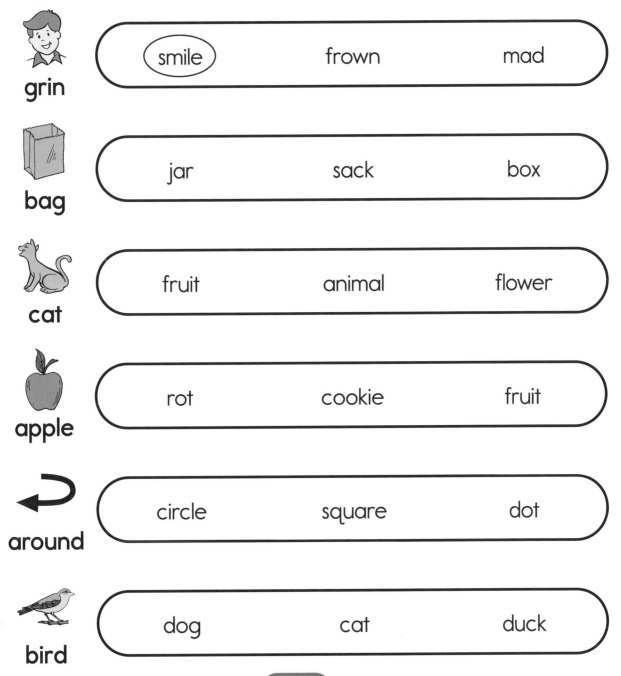

grin — smile   frown   mad

bag — jar   sack   box

cat — fruit   animal   flower

apple — rot   cookie   fruit

around — circle   square   dot

bird — dog   cat   duck

A Synonym Story

Directions: Read the story. Write a word on the line that means almost the same as the word under the line.

Dan went to the _____.
store

He wanted to buy _____.
food

He walked very _____.
quickly

The store had what he wanted.

He bought it using _____.
dimes

Instead of walking home, Dan _____.
jogged

102

All About Antonyms

Antonyms are words that are opposites. **Hot** and **cold** are antonyms.

Directions: Draw a line between the antonyms.

closed

below

full

empty

above

old

new

open

Name _____

Opposites Attract

Directions: Circle the picture in each row that is the opposite of the first picture.

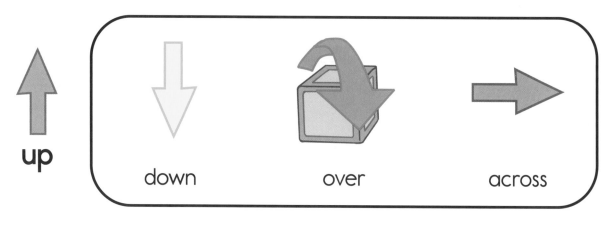

up

down   over   across

cold

frozen   hot   warm

cloud

rain   storm   sun

Fishing for Antonyms

Directions: Read each clue. Write the answers in the puzzle.

high   yes   left
heavy   tight
safe   full

Across:

1. Opposite of low
2. Opposite of no
4. Opposite of empty
6. Opposite of loose

Down:

1. Opposite of light
3. Opposite of dangerous
5. Opposite of right

Sound Alikes

Homophones are words that **sound** the same but are spelled differently and mean something different. **Blew** and **blue** are homophones.

Directions: Look at the word pairs. Choose the word that describes the picture. Write the word on the line next to the picture.

1. sew   so   _____

2. pair   pear   _____

3. eye   I   _____

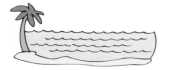

4. see   sea   _____

Sound Alikes

Directions: Read each sentence. Underline the two words that sound the same but are spelled differently and mean something different.

1. Tom ate eight grapes.

2. Becky read *Little Red Riding Hood.*

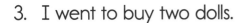

3. I went to buy two dolls.

4. Five blue feathers blew in the wind.

5. Would you get wood for the fire?

Say it with a Sentence

Sentences begin with capital letters.

Directions: Read the sentences and write them below. Begin each sentence with a capital letter.

Example:

the cat is fat.

The cat is fat.

my dog is big.

_____

- - - - - - - - - - - - - - -

_____

the boy is sad.

_____

- - - - - - - - - - - - - - -

_____

bikes are fun!

_____

- - - - - - - - - - - - - - -

_____

dad can bake.

_____

- - - - - - - - - - - - - - -

_____

All in Order

If you change the order of the words in a sentence, you can change the meaning of a sentence.

Directions: Read the sentences. Draw a circle around the sentence that describes the picture.

Example:

(The fox jumped over the dogs.)

The dogs jumped over the fox.

1. The cat watched the bird.

    The bird watched the cat.

2. The girl looked at the boy.

    The boy looked at the girl.

3. The turtle ran past the rabbit.

    The rabbit ran past the turtle.

Name _____

Lemonade for Sale!

Directions: Look at the picture. Put the words in order. Write the sentences on the lines below.

1. We made lemonade. some

2. good. It was

3. We the sold lemonade.

4. cost It five cents.

5. fun. We had

1. _____

2. _____

3. _____

4. _____

5. _____

Telling Sentences: Pet Crazy

Directions: Read the sentences and write them below. Begin each sentence with a capital letter. End each sentence with a period.

1. most children like pets
2. some children like dogs
3. some children like cats
4. some children like snakes
5. some children like all animals

1. _____

2. _____

3. _____

4. _____

5. _____

Telling Sentences: Going Shopping

Directions: Read the sentences and write them below. Begin each sentence with a capital letter. End each sentence with a period.

1. i like to go to the store with Mom
2. we go on Friday
3. i get to push the cart
4. i get to buy the cookies
5. I like to help Mom

1. _____

2. _____

3. _____

4. _____

5. _____

Asking Sentences: Monkeying Around

Directions: Write the first word of each asking sentence. Be sure to begin each question with a capital letter. End each question with a question mark.

1. _____ you like the zoo   do

2. _____ much does it cost   how

3. _____ you feed the ducks   can

4. _____ you see the monkeys   will

5. _____ time will you eat lunch   what

Asking Sentences: Getting to Know You

Directions: Read the asking sentences. Write the sentences below. Begin each sentence with a capital letter. End each sentence with a question mark.

1. what game will we play
2. do you like to read
3. how old are you

4. who is your best friend
5. can you tie your shoes

1. _____

2. _____

3. _____

4. _____

5. _____

Punctuation Parade

Directions: Put a period or a question mark at the end of each sentence below.

1. Do you like parades

2. The clowns lead the parade

3. Can you hear the band

4. The balloons are big

5. Can you see the horses

Review

Directions: Look at the picture. In the space below, write one telling sentence about the picture. Then, write one asking sentence about the picture.

Telling sentence:

_____

- -

_____

_____

- -

_____

Asking sentence:

_____

- -

_____

_____

- -

Busy, Busy Animals

Directions: Use the words in the pictures to write a sentence about each animal. Put a period at the end of each sentence.

Example:

The  eats bugs.

The frog eats bugs.

The drinks milk

The eats seeds

The  jumps out

The  meet

121

Name _____

From Here to There

Directions: Trace the letters to write the name of each thing. Write each name again by yourself. Then, color the pictures.

Example:

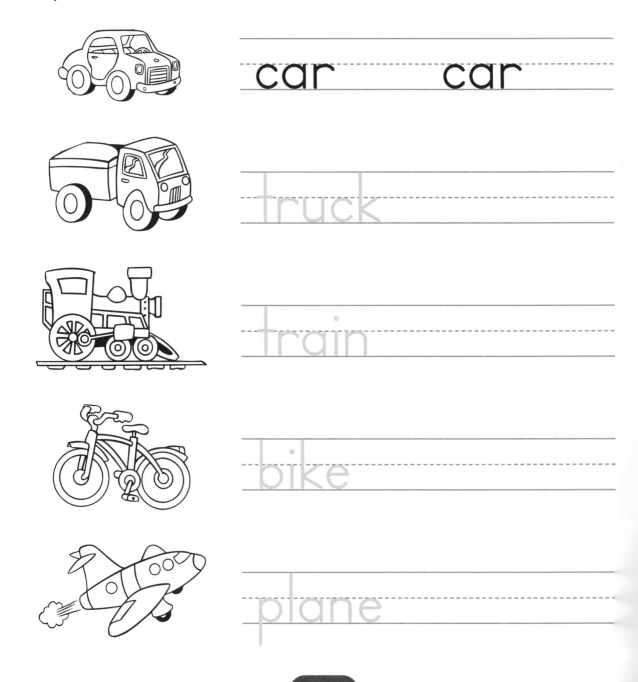

car   car

truck

train

bike

plane

On the Go

Directions: Say the name of each thing. Write the beginning sound under its name. Find two pictures in each row that begin with the same sound as the first picture. Write the same first letter under them.

Example:

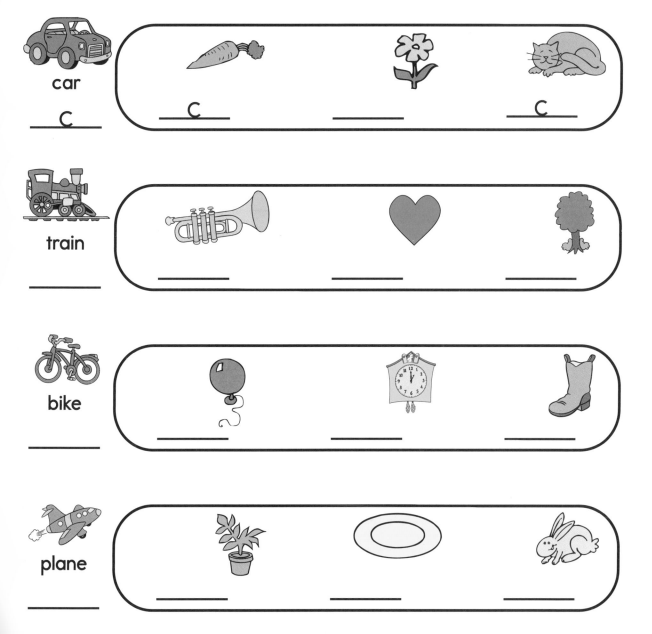

Name _____

Time to Get Dressed

Directions: Trace the letters to write the name of each clothing word. Then, write each name again by yourself.

Example:

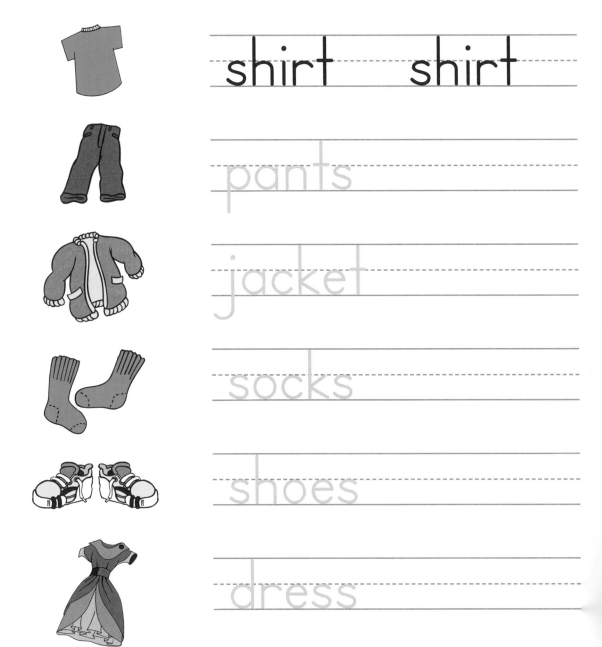

shirt   shirt

pants

jacket

socks

shoes

dress

Matching Clothes

Directions: Some of these sentences tell a whole idea. Others have something missing. If something is missing, draw a line to the word that completes the sentence. Put a period at the end of each sentence.

Example:

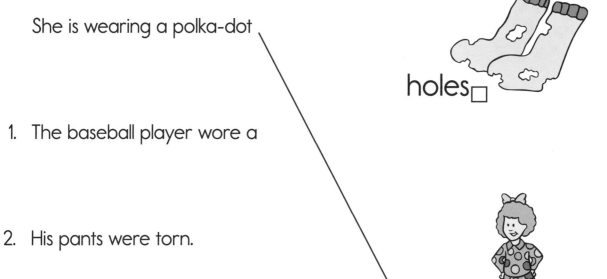

She is wearing a polka-dot

holes☐

1. The baseball player wore a

2. His pants were torn.

dress◉

3. The socks had

4. The jacket had blue buttons.

hat☐

5. The shoes were brown.

A Bite to Eat

Directions: Trace the letters to write the name of each food word. Write each name again by yourself. Then, color the pictures.

Example:

bread bread

cookie

apple

cake

milk

egg

Name _____

Spelling in Action

To show more than one of something, add **s** to the end of the word.

Example: one cat   two cats

Directions: In each sentence, add **s** to show more than one. Then, write the action word that completes each sentence.

| sit | jump | stop | ride |

Example:

The frog __s__ __sleep__ in the sun.

1. The boy __ _____ on the fence.

2. The car __ _____ at the sign.

3. The girl __ _____ in the water.

4. The dog __ _____ in the wagon.

Makes Sense to Me!

Directions: Circle the word that is spelled correctly. Then, write the correct spelling in the blank.

Example:

tast

(taste)

tste

taste

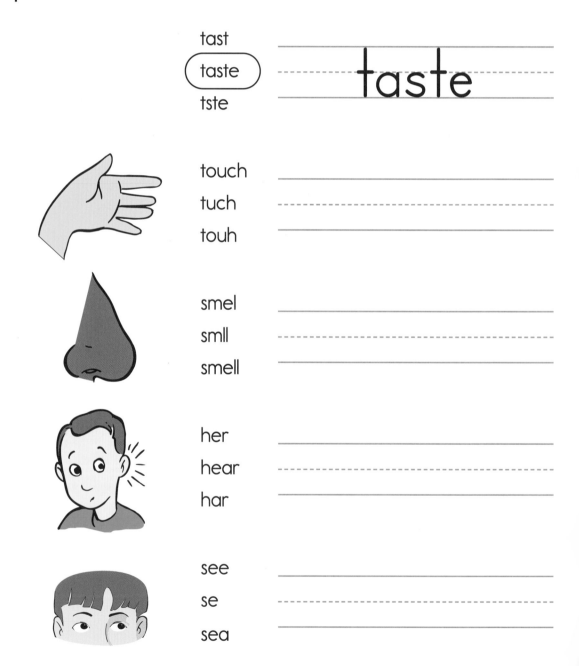

touch

tuch

touh

smel

smll

smell

her

hear

har

see

se

sea

Makes Sense to Me!

Directions: Use the sense words in the box to answer each question.

> smell   see   taste   hear   touch

1. Which word begins with the same sound as ?

   _____

   -

   _____

2. Which word begins with the same sound as ?

   _____

   -

   _____

3. Which words begin with the same sound as ?

   _____   _____

   - - - - - - - - - - - - - - - -   - - - - - - - - - - - - - - - - - - -

   _____   _____

4. Which word begins with the same sound as ?

   _____

   -

   _____

How's the Weather?

Directions: Write the weather word that completes each sentence. Put a period at the end of the telling sentences and a question mark at the end of the asking sentences.

Example:

Do flowers grow in the ____ **sun** ____ [?]

| rain | water | wet | hot |

1. The sun makes me _____ [ ]

2. When it rains, the grass gets _____ [ ]

3. Do you think it will _____ on our picnic [ ]

4. Should you drink the _____ from the rain [ ]

How's the Weather?

Directions: Write the missing words to complete the story. The first letter of each word is written for you.

"Please may I go outside?" I asked.

"It's too C _____," my father told me. "Maybe

later the sun will come out." Later, the sun did come out.

Then, it began to r _____ again. "May I go

out now?" I asked again. Dad looked out the window.

"You will get W _____," he said. "But I want to

see if the r _____ helped our flowers grow,"

I said. "You mean you want to play in the W _____,"

Dad said with a smile. How did Dad know that?

Head to Toe

Directions: Write the word that completes each sentence. Put a period at the end of the telling sentences and a question mark at the end of the asking sentences.

Example:

I wear my hat on my ___ **head** ___ .

arms   legs   feet   hands

1. How strong are your _____

2. You wear shoes on your _____

3. If you're happy and you know it, clap your

   _____

4. My pants covered my _____

Head to Toe

Directions: Read the sentence parts below. Draw a line from the first part of the sentence to the second part that completes it.

1. I give big hugs

with my arms.

with my car.

2. My feet

drive the car.

got wet in the rain.

3. I have a bump

on my head.

on my coat.

4. My mittens

keep my arms warm.

keep my hands warm.

5. I can jump high

using my legs.

using a spoon.

What's the Difference?

Some words are opposites. **Opposites** are things that are different in every way. **Dark** and **light** are opposites.

Directions: Trace the letters to write each word. Then, write the word again by yourself.

Example:

new   new

old

big

little

lost

found

What's the Difference?

Directions: Read the sentence about the first picture. Write another sentence about the picture beside it. Use the opposite words.

Example:

This apple is little.

 This apple is big.

dark   old   first   new   light   last

1. This coat is light.

 _____

2. This woman is first.

 _____

3. This car is old.

 _____

Name _____

People Power!

Directions: Trace the letters to write each word. Then, write the word again by yourself.

girl

boy

man

woman

people

children

People Power!

Sometimes we use other words in place of people names. For **boy** or **man**, we can use the word **he**. For **girl** or **woman**, we can use the word **she**. For two or more people, we can use the word **they**.

Directions: Write the words **he**, **she**, or **they** in these sentences.

Example:

The boy likes cookies.

 He _____ likes cookies.

1. The girl is running fast.

   _____

   _____ is running fast.

2. The man reads the paper.

   _____

   _____ reads the paper.

3. The woman has a cold.

   _____

   _____ has a cold.

4. Two children came to school.

   _____

   _____ came to school.

People Power!

Directions: Write the people word that completes each sentence.

> man   woman   boy   children   girl

1. The _____ feeds the cat.

2. The _____ are buying dessert.

3. What is the _____ painting?

4. The _____ will grow corn.

5. The dog runs to the _____.

Math

Know Your Numbers

Directions: Use the color codes to color the parrot.

Color:

1's red

2's blue

3's yellow

4's green

5's orange

144

Hop to It!

Directions: How many are there of each picture? Write the answers in the boxes. The first one is done for you.

Counting Zoo

Directions: How many are there of each shape? Write the answers in the boxes. The first one is done for you.

Add It Up: 1–2

Addition means "putting together," or adding, two or more numbers to find the sum. "+" is a plus sign. It means to add the 2 numbers. "=" is an equals sign. It tells how much they are together.

Directions: Count the cats and tell how many.

Name _____

Add It Up: 3–6

Directions: Practice writing the numbers and then add. Draw dots to help, if needed.

3

4

5

6

$$2 \cdot\cdot$$
$$+4 \cdot\cdot\cdot\cdot$$
___

$$1$$
$$+4$$
___

$$3$$
$$+2$$
___

$$1$$
$$+2$$
___

Add It Up: 6–8

Directions: Practice writing the numbers and then add. Draw dots to help, if needed.

6

7

8 _____

$$3$$
$$+4$$
————

$$5$$
$$+1$$
————

$$2$$
$$+6$$
————

$$4$$
$$+4$$
————

Add It Up: 7–9

Directions: Practice writing the numbers and then add. Draw dots to help, if needed.

7 _____

8 _____

9 _____

$$\begin{array}{r} 8 \\ +1 \\ \hline \end{array}$$ $$\begin{array}{r} 3 \\ +5 \\ \hline \end{array}$$ $$\begin{array}{r} 2 \\ +7 \\ \hline \end{array}$$ $$\begin{array}{r} 6 \\ +1 \\ \hline \end{array}$$

In the Doghouse

Directions: Add the numbers. Put your answers in the doghouses.

Example: $4 + 2 =$  6

$2 + 6 =$

$7 + 3 =$

$6 + 1 =$

$4 + 5 =$

$6 + 2 =$

$7 + 2 =$

Subtraction Action: 1–3

Subtraction means "taking away," or subtracting, one number from another. "–" is a minus sign. It means to subtract the second number from the first.

Directions: Practice writing the numbers and then subtract. Draw dots and cross them out, if needed.

1 _____

2 _____

3 _____

$$3 - 1 = 2$$

$$4 - 3$$

$$2 - 1$$

$$3 - 2$$

Picture This: Addition

Directions: Solve the number problem under each picture.

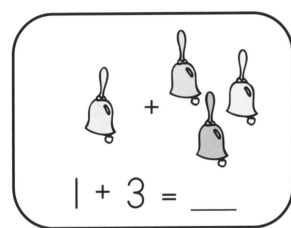

1 + 3 = ___

2 + 4 = ___

3 + 5 = ___

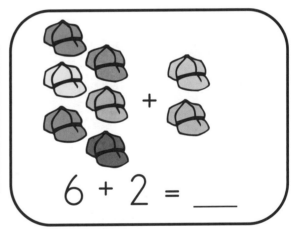

6 + 2 = ___

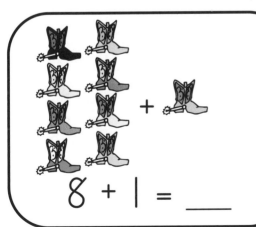

8 + 1 = ___

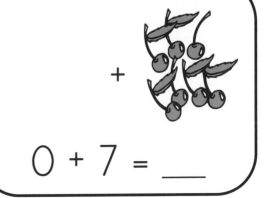

0 + 7 = ___

MATH

Name _____

Picture This: Subtraction

Directions: Solve the number problem under each picture.

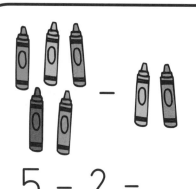

5 – 2 = ___

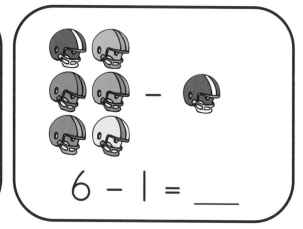

6 – 1 = ___

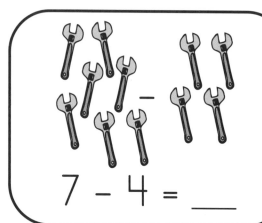

7 – 4 = ___

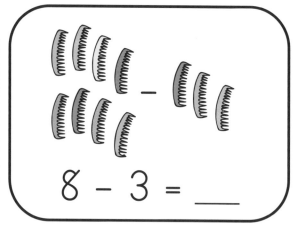

8 – 3 = ___

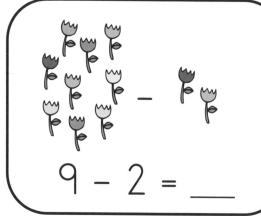

9 – 2 = ___

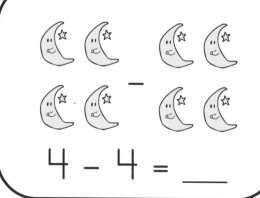

4 – 4 = ___

Skip by Tens

Directions: Count in order by tens to draw the path the boy takes to the store.

Name ______________________________

Counting on Crayons

Directions: Circle groups of ten crayons. Add the remaining ones to make the correct number.

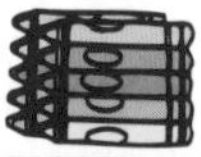 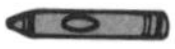 **tens ones**

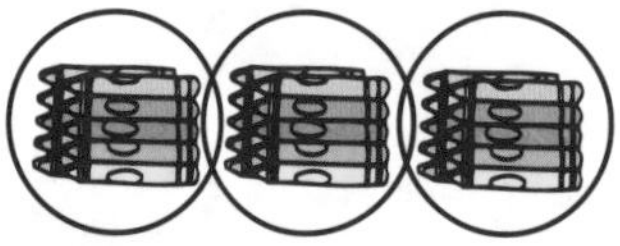 + 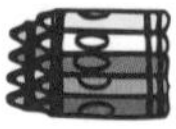 = 3 9

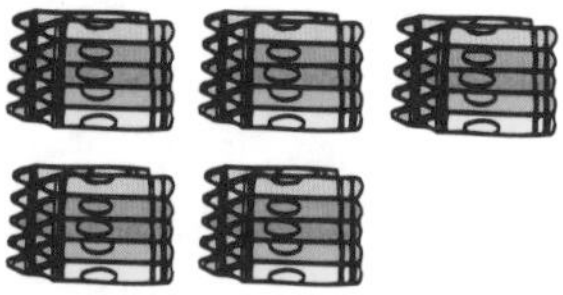 + 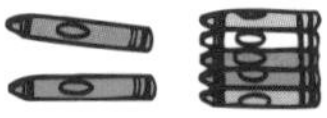 = ___ ___

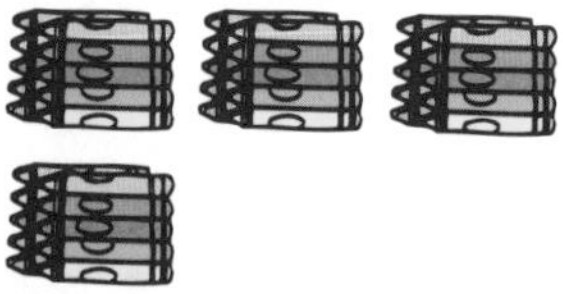 + 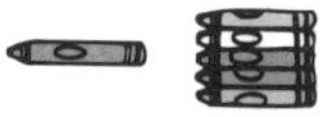 = ___ ___

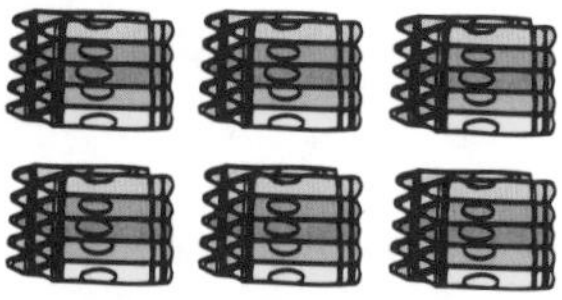 + 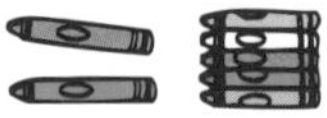 = ___ ___

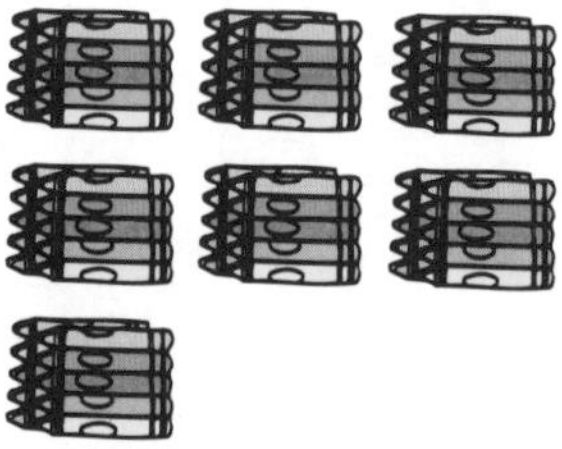 + 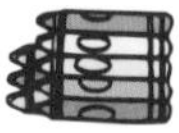 = ___ ___

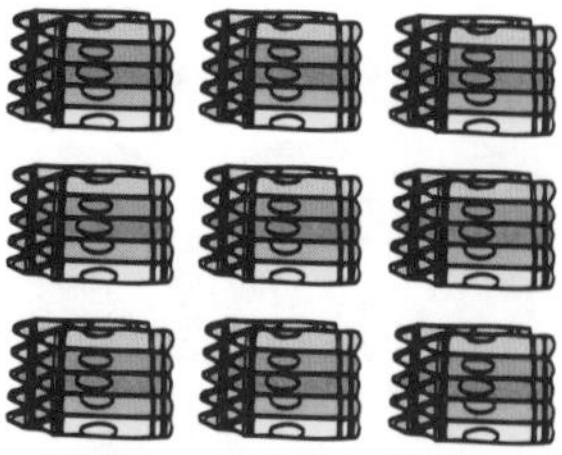 + 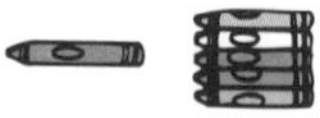 = ___ ___

6 + 6 = ___ 8 + 4 = ___ 9 + 5 = ___

Crayon Cross-out

Directions: Count the crayons in each group. Put an **X** through the number of crayons being subtracted. How many are left?

15 – 5 = __10__

– 4 = ___

– 7 = ___

– 6 = ___

– 5 = ___

– 8 = ___

13 – 8 = ___   11 – 5 = ___   12 – 9 = ___

14 – 7 = ___   10 – 7 = ___   13 – 3 = ___

15 – 9 = ___   11 – 8 = ___   12 – 10 = ___

Fair and Square

A square is a figure with four corners and four sides of the same length. This is a square ☐.

Directions: Find the squares and circle them.

Directions: Trace the word. Write the word.

square

Circles All Around

A circle is a figure that is round. This is a circle ○.

Directions: Find the circles and put a square around them.

Directions: Trace the word. Write the word.

circle

Totally Triangles

A triangle is a figure with three corners and three sides. This is a triangle △.

Directions: Find the triangles and put a circle around them.

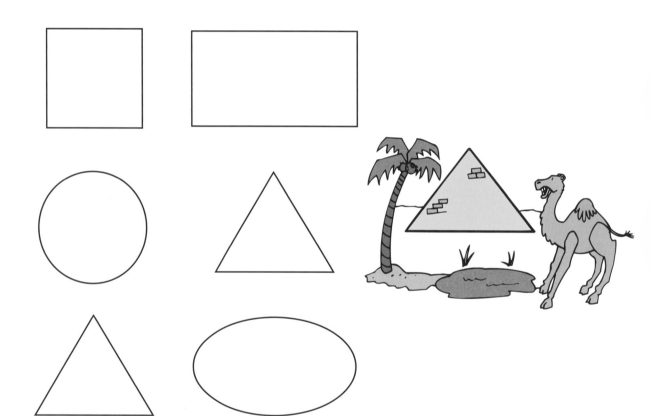

Directions: Trace the word. Write the word.

triangle _____

Make Room for Rectangles

A rectangle is a figure with four corners and four sides. Sides opposite each other are the same length. This is a rectangle ▭.

Directions: Find the rectangles and put a circle around them.

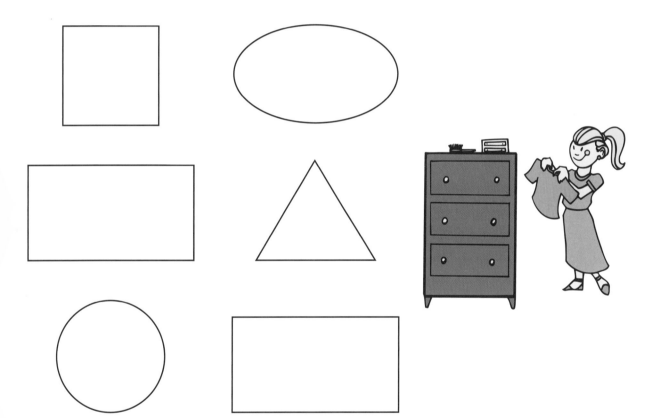

Directions: Trace the word. Write the word.

rectangle

Ovals and Rhombuses

An oval is an egg-shaped figure. A rhombus is a figure with four sides of the same length. It's corners form points at the top, sides and bottom. This is an oval ⬭. This is a rhombus ◇.

Directions: Color the ovals **red**. Color the rhombuses **blue**.

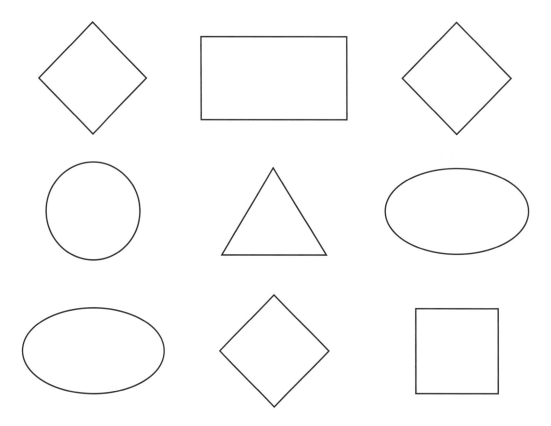

Directions: Trace the word. Write the word.

oval

rhombus

Shape Up

Directions: Look at the shapes. Answer the questions.

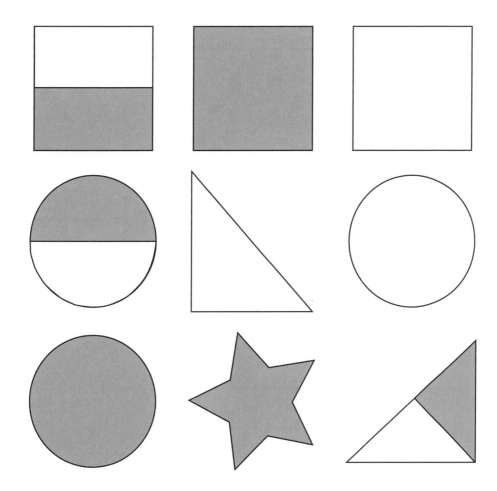

1. How many all-white shapes? _____

2. How many all-blue shapes? _____

3. How many half-white shapes? _____

4. How many all-blue stars? _____

5. How many all-white circles? _____

6. How many half-blue shapes? _____

Name _____

Ship Shape

Directions: Draw an **X** on the shapes in each row that do not match the first shape.

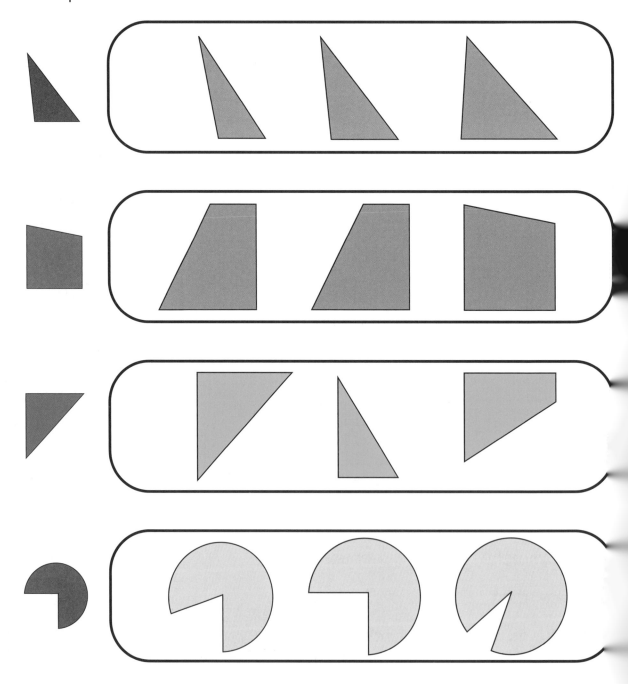

Name _____

Pattern Play

Directions: Draw a line from the box on the left to the box on the right with the same shape and color pattern.

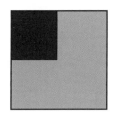

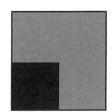

Name _____

Pattern Play

Directions: Circle the shape in the middle box that matches the one on the left. Draw another shape with the same pattern in the box on the right.

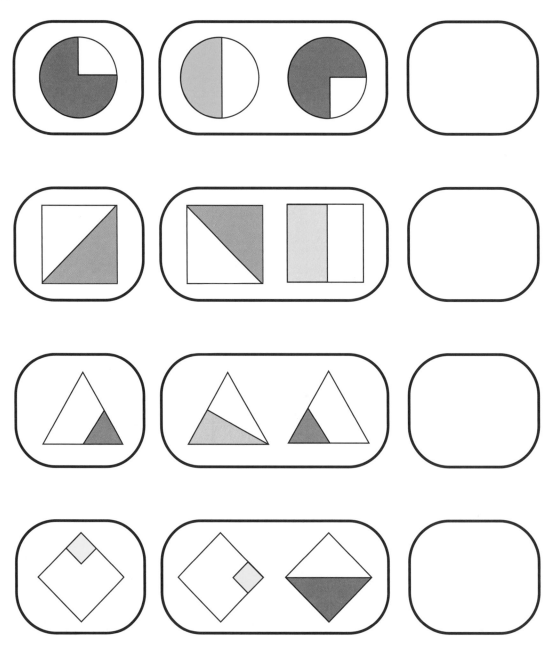

Pattern Play

Directions: Fill in the missing shape in each row. Then, color it.

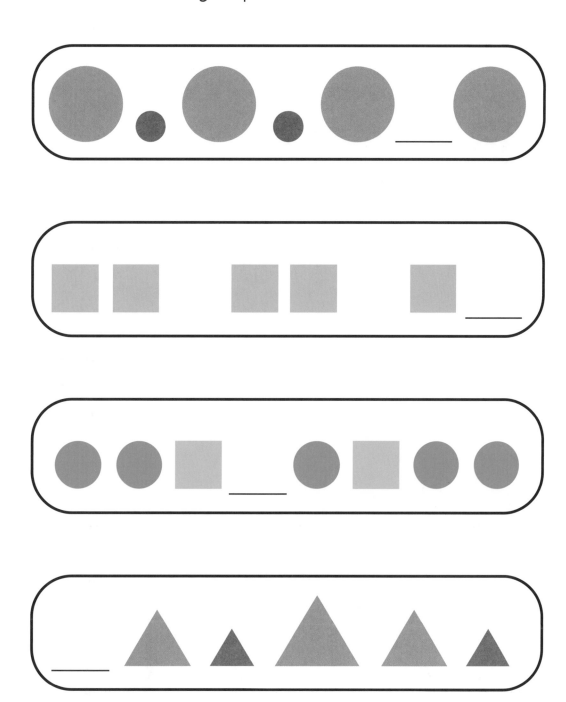

Fraction Action: Whole and Half

A fraction is a number that names part of a whole, such as $\frac{1}{2}$ or $\frac{3}{4}$.

Directions: Color half of each object.

Example:

$\frac{1}{2}$

Whole apple   **Half an apple**

Fraction Action: Halves $\frac{1}{2}$

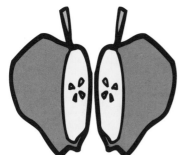

$\frac{1}{2}$ $\dfrac{\text{Part shaded or divided}}{\text{Number of equal parts.}}$

Directions: Color only the shapes that show halves.

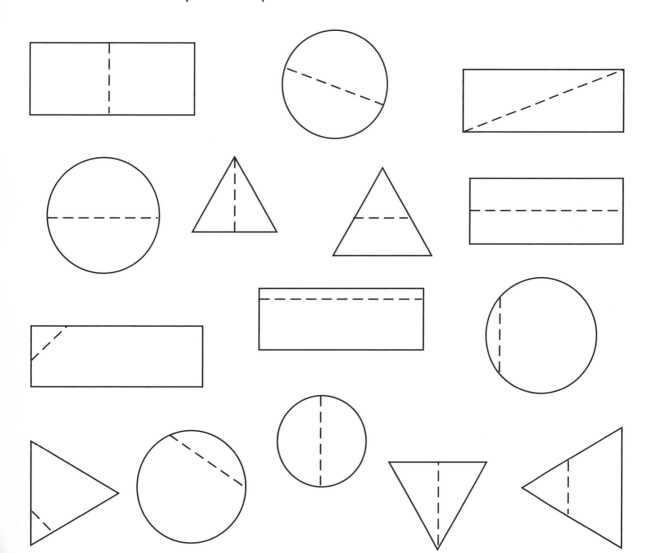

Name _____

Fraction Action: Thirds and Fourths

Directions: Each object has 3 equal parts. Color one section.

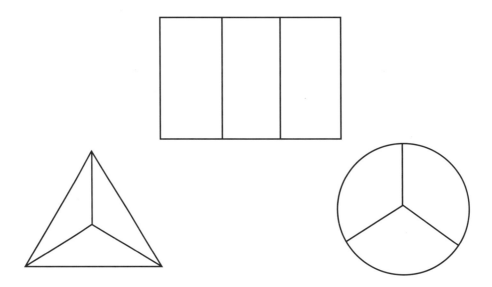

Directions: Each object has 4 equal parts. Color one section.

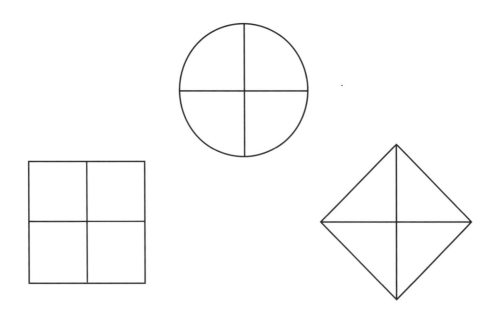

Review

Directions: Count the equal parts, then write the fraction.

Example:

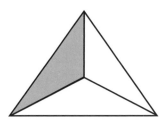

Shaded part   =   __1__

Equal parts   =   __3__

Write $\dfrac{1}{3}$

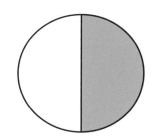

Shaded part   =   __1__

Equal parts   =   _____

Write   __

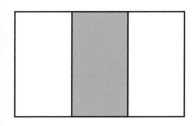

Shaded part   =   __1__

Equal parts   =   _____

Write   __

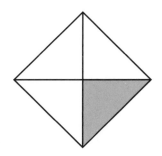

Shaded part   =   __1__

Equal parts   =   _____

Write   __

Name _____

On the Right Track

Directions: Draw a straight line from A to B. Use a different color crayon for each line.

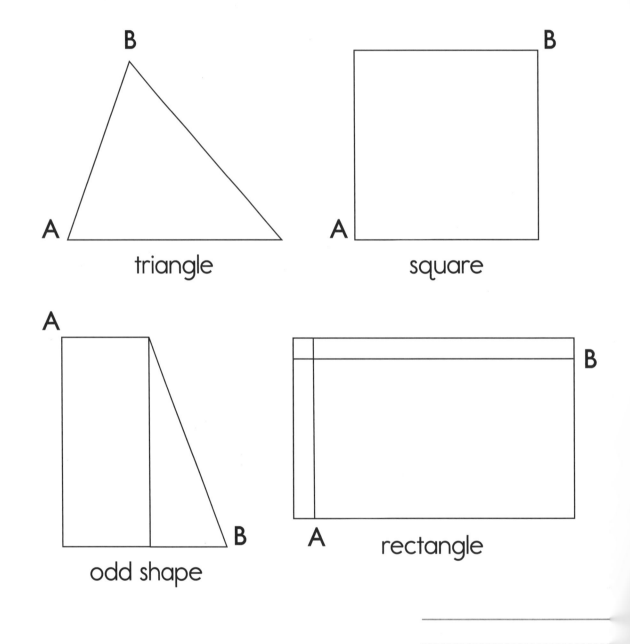

What shapes do you see hidden in these shapes? _____

_____

Inch by Inch

A ruler has 12 inches. 12 inches equal 1 foot.

Directions: Cut out the ruler at the bottom of the page. Measure the objects to the nearest inch.

The screwdriver is _____ inches long.

The pencil is _____ inches long.

The pen is _____ inches long.

The fork is _____ inches long.

Cut ✄---

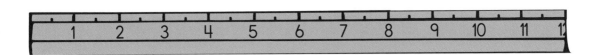

This page is blank for the cutting activity
on the opposite side.

Abbreviation: A short way of writing words. **Examples:** Mon., Tues., etc.

Addition: "Putting together" or adding two or more numbers to find the sum.

Alphabetical (ABC) Order: Putting letters or words in the order in which they appear in the alphabet.

Antonyms: Words that are opposites. **Example:** big and small are opposites.

Asking Sentences: Sentences that ask a question. An asking sentence begins with a capital letter and ends with a question mark.

Beginning Consonants: Consonant sounds that come at the beginning of words.

Beginning Sounds: The sounds you hear first in a word.

Capital Letters: Letters that are used at the beginning of names of people, places, days, months and holidays. Capital letters are also used at the beginning of sentences. These letters (A, B, C, D, E, F, G, H, I, J, K, L, M, N, O, P, Q, R, S, T, U, V, W, X, Y and Z) are sometimes called uppercase or "big" letters.

Circle: A figure that is round. It looks like this: ◯

Classifying: Putting objects, words or ideas that are alike into categories.

Compound Words: Two words that are put together to make one new word. **Example:** house + boat = houseboat.

Comprehension: Understanding what is seen, heard or read.

Consonant Blends: Two consonant sounds put together.

Consonants: The letters b, c, d, f, g, h, j, k, l, m, n, p, q, r, s, t, v, w, x, y and z. Consonants are all the letters except a, e, i, o and u.

Describing Words: Words that tell more about a person, place or thing.

Diamond: A figure with four sides of the same length. Its corners form points at the top, sides and bottom. It looks like this: ◇

Digits: The symbols used to write numbers: 0, 1, 2, 3, 4, 5, 6, 7, 8 and 9.

Dime: Ten cents. It is written 10¢ or $.10.

Directions: Doing what the instructions say to do.

Ending Consonants: Consonant sounds which come at the end of words.

Ending Sounds: The sounds made by the last letters of words.

Following Directions: Doing what the directions say to do.

Fraction: A number that names part of a whole, such as $\frac{1}{2}$ or $\frac{2}{3}$.

Half-Hour: Thirty minutes. When the long hand of the clock is pointing to the six, the time is on the half-hour. It is written :30, such as 5:30.

Homophones: Words that sound the same but are spelled differently and mean different things. **Example:** blue and blew.

Hour: Sixty minutes. The short hand of a clock tells the hour. It is written 2:00.

Long Vowels: The letters a, e, i, o and u which say the "long" or letter name sound. Long a is the sound you hear in hay. Long e is the sound you hear in me. Long i is the sound you hear in pie. Long o is the sound you hear in no. Long u is the sound you hear in cute.

Making Inferences: Using logic to figure out what is unspoken but known to be true.

Nickel: Five cents. It is written 5¢ or $.05.

Nouns: Name a person, place or thing.

Opposites: Things that are different in every way.

Ordinal Numbers: Numbers that indicate order in a series, such as first, second or third.

Oval: A figure that is egg-shaped. It looks like this: ◯

Pattern: A repeated arrangement of pictures, letters or shapes.

Penny: One cent. It is written 1¢ or $.01.

Period: Tells you when to stop reading and is found at the end of sentences. It looks like this: .

Picture Clues: Looking at the pictures to figure out meaning.

Place Value: The value of a digit, or numeral, shown by where it is in the number. For example, in the number 23, 2 has the place value of tens and 3 is ones.

Predicting: Telling what is likely to happen based on available facts.

Rectangle: A figure with four corners and four sides. Sides opposite each other are the same length. It looks like this: ▭

Rhymes: Words with the same ending sounds.

Rhyming Words: Words that sound alike at the end of the word. **Example:** cat and rat.

Same and Different: Being able to tell how things are alike and not alike.

Sentence: A group of words that tells a complete idea.

Sequencing: Putting numbers in the correct order, such as 7, 8, 9.

Short Vowels: The letters a, e, i, o and u which say the short sound. Short a is the sound you hear in ant. Short e is the sound you hear in elephant. Short i is the sound you hear in igloo. Short o is the sound you hear in octopus. Short u is the sound you hear in umbrella.

Similar: Things that are almost the same.

Square: A figure with four corners and four sides of the same length. It looks like this: ☐

Subtraction: "Taking away" or subtracting one number from another. For example: 10 – 3 = 7.

Super Silent E: The e that is added to some words which changes the short vowel sound to a long vowel sound. **Example:** rip + e = ripe.

Synonyms: Words that mean the same thing. **Example:** small and little.

Telling Sentences: Sentences that tell something. A telling sentence begins with a capital letter and ends with a period.

Tracking: Following a path.

Triangle: A figure with three corners and three sides. It looks like this: △

Verbs: Words that tell what a person or thing can do.

Vowels: The letters a, e, i, o, u and sometimes y.

Addition

Make your own "plus" sign. Glue two toothpicks or popsicle sticks together. Then, your child can create groups of objects on either side of the "plus" sign to add.

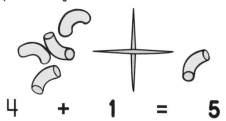

4   +   1   =   5

Use dry beans or other small objects to practice counting. Have your child divide ten beans into two separate groups and combine them by adding. Have your child write the number problem on paper and read it to you.

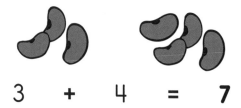

3   +   4   =   7

Look through magazines with your child. Encourage them to create addition problems from the pictures. For example: "One Mommy plus two children equals three!"

Alphabetical (ABC) Order

Write three or four words (names of family members, color words, objects found in the kitchen) on a sheet of paper. Space them so they can be cut out and rearranged in random order. Have your child move them around so that they are in the correct order. At first, you will need to be careful not to include two words that begin with the same letter. As your child masters ABC order, however, you can show them how to use the second letter of a word when doing alphabetical order. Words such as "brown" and "blue" both begin with the letter "b," so your child would need to look at the "r" and the "l" to help them determine which word would come first.

Give your child a copy of your weekly grocery list, and let them rewrite it for you in alphabetical order.

Show your child a dictionary. Lead them to discover that the words are listed in alphabetical order. Purchase an inexpensive picture dictionary for your child to use in their writing, and encourage them to "look up" words they want to spell correctly.

Classifying

Classifying involves putting objects, words or ideas that are alike into categories. Objects can be classified in more than one way. For example, hats could be sorted by size, color or season worn. If your child creates a category you had not considered, praise them for thinking creatively.

Your child could sort the clothing in their closet. They could sort it according to the season each item is worn, by color, type of clothing or even likes and dislikes. You can also have your child help you sort laundry.

At the grocery store, talk about the layout of the store and how items are arranged. For example, fruits are together, vegetables are together, cooking supplies are together, soups are together, etc. Talk about why items would be arranged in groups like that. What would happen if they were not arranged in groups? Have your child help you find what you need by having them decide what section of the store it would be in. After finding the item, talk about alternate places the item could be found.

When planning a family vacation, collect travel brochures on possible destinations and sites to see. Have your child classify the brochures according to location, activity or places you may or may not want to visit. Use these groupings to plan your trip.

Recycling is a good way to practice classifying. Label recycling containers clearly (paper, plastic, glass, metal). Your child's job can be to sort the recyclables and put them in the correct containers.

Let your child help you organize the kitchen cupboards, a closet or dresser drawer. Food could be organized into food groups. Clothes and shoes could be sorted by season or color.

Help your child take a poll while riding in the car. Decide on a topic (color of cars, types of vehicles seen, color of houses, etc.). Have your child draw columns on a sheet of paper and label the columns. Each time you or your child spots an object that belongs in a category, have them make a tally mark in that column.

Encourage your child to help you as you prepare meals in the kitchen. Talk about the places where kitchen utensils are kept—silverware, glasses, plates, etc. As you dry the dishes or empty the dishwasher, your child can sort the forks, spoons and knives or the plates and glasses. Helping to sort and fold the laundry is another practical way to reinforce this skill.

Arrange an assortment of "like" objects, such as buttons, safety pins, paper clips (all used to fasten things) or chalk, pens, markers (things used to write with), and have your child find something that also belongs in that grouping. You could also arrange an assortment of "like" materials with one object that doesn't belong and have your child remove the wrong one.

Colors

Fill six clear plastic glasses half full with water. Have your child experiment with mixing drops of food coloring into each cup. Talk about the colors created and how they were created. Help your child record their findings. For example, red + yellow = orange.

THINGS THAT FASTEN

Compound Words

Look for compound words in newspapers and magazines or write compound words on cards, and cut them apart for your child. Challenge your child to match the word parts, glue them together and illustrate them.

Comprehension

Your child can make a poster for a book or movie. Have them include the important events, the most exciting parts, their favorite part and reasons why someone else should view or read it.

Comprehension involves understanding what is seen, heard or read. To help your child with this skill, talk about a book, picture, movie or television program. Ask your child if they like it and the reasons why or why not. By listening to what they say, you can tell whether the book, etc. was understood. If your child does not fully understand part of it, discuss that section further. Reread the book or watch the program again, if possible.

Watch the news with your child and discuss the job of a news reporter. After your child understands what reporters do, create your own newscast. You can be the reporter, and your child can pretend to be a character from a book or movie. Make up the questions together, based on a book they have read or a movie they have watched. Use the questions for an "interview." If you have a video camera, record your interview, and play it back for your child to watch.

After reading a book, have your child create a book cover for it. The picture should tell about the book and include a brief summary on the back. If the book belongs to your child, they could use the cover on the book.

Find a comic strip without words or use a comic strip from the newspaper and cut off the words. Have your child look at the pictures and create words to go along with them. If your child has difficulty writing, you may want to write what they say.

Consonants/Vowels

Have your child write the names of family members and graph the number of consonants and vowels in each person's name. Then ask questions to help your child interpret the graph. For example: "Whose name has the most vowels?" "The most consonants?" "Whose name has the most letters?"

Play "Letter Bingo" or "Word Bingo" with your child. Cut pictures from magazines and glue them on a Bingo board. Start by calling out beginning consonant sounds. For example, "Cover words that start with the letter 't.'" You can make the game more difficult by asking your child to identify words by both their beginning and ending sound, as in "Cover the word that begins with a 't' and ends with a 'd.' "

Have your child brainstorm a list of words that have the short a sound (or whatever vowel you're working on) in the beginning or middle. Looking at pictures in books or magazines may help spark ideas.

Counting

Have your child write their name. Have them count the number of letters in their name and the number of times each letter appears. Have your child do the same with your name and other family members' names.

Buy or make a calendar for your child to keep in their room. Have your child number the calendar. Put stickers on or draw pictures to mark special days. Have your child cross out each day.

Play the card game "War" with your child. Each player needs an equal number of cards. Explain the value of face cards to your child. Each player places a card facedown and turns it over at the same time. The player with the higher number gets to keep both cards.

Following Directions

Give your child a set of three directions to follow. For example, you could say, "Go to the refrigerator and get a carrot stick. Put it on a small plate. Take it to your father in the garage." You may be able to increase the steps in the sequence, but do not make the skill so difficult that your child gets frustrated. Then, reverse your roles! Have your child give you a set of directions to follow. This change is not only fun for them, it is also good practice in giving clear directions.

When playing a new game, read the directions with your child. Then have them explain how to play the game. When a friend visits, let your child explain the rules of the game.

Write a note for your child, giving step-by-step directions on how to do something. If they cannot read yet, use pictures to show what needs to be done. Encourage your child to follow the directions to complete the task.

Fractions

Let your child help you cut pie or pizza into equal slices.

Peel an orange. Separate the sections and talk about "fractions" as parts of a whole.

Pick clovers. Talk about equal parts as you pull off the petals.

Fold a sheet of paper into four equal sections. Have your child shade three sections blue and one brown. Explain that $\frac{3}{4}$ of the Earth is water and $\frac{1}{4}$ is land.

Letter Sounds

Write each consonant letter on a large index card. Choose four to eight of the cards and lay them out on a table. Say a word that begins with one of the letters and have your child identify the beginning sound. (At first, avoid naming words that begin with blends and digraphs such as frog or shop.) Repeat with other consonant letters.

To help your child develop his/her skill in recognizing beginning and ending sounds, play a game of "I Spy" together. Say, for example, "I see something in this room that starts with the sound of 't,'" or "I spy something that ends with the same sound as 'top.'" Your child should respond with an appropriate object. You can make the game more challenging by using consonant blends, as in "Can you spy something that begins with the same beginning blend as 'glove'?"

Make up letter riddles. **Example:** "I'm thinking of an animal that hops and whose name begins with 'r.'" Have your child guess the answer.

Letter Sounds and ABC Order

Create an ABC scavenger hunt for your child. Provide your child with a list of words and pictures representing each of the 26 letters of the alphabet.
For example:

a   apple

b   ball

c   cat

d   doll

Let them collect the items for the scavenger hunt from around your home or neighborhood and label them.

Letter Recognition and Formation

Use glue to "write" the capital and lowercase letters of the alphabet. After the glue dries, encourage your child to trace the letters with their fingers. Then encourage them to identify the letters with their eyes closed!

Using white liquid glue, have your child "write" words in large letters on drawing paper. Then, have your child place thick yarn in the glue to form each letter of the word. When the words dry, your child can trace them with their fingers while spelling the words.

On a trip to the beach, encourage your child to write the entire alphabet in the sand before the waves wash the letters away!

Making Inferences

Talk about daily events with your child. Ask your child questions about what they think might happen next or how a person might have felt about an event. Ask your child how they arrived at that answer.

Use questions to encourage your child to think about why people do things. For example, "Why do you think that man is scraping the paint off the house?" "Why do you think we are buying chicken at the store today?" Based upon what your child sees, they can come up with information without being told.

Measurement

Purchase a plastic or wooden ruler for your child. Let them measure various objects around the house. Record their findings and talk about length.

Money

Practice counting by fives with nickels and by tens with dimes.

Let your child label canned goods in your home with "prices." They will gain valuable practice counting and exchanging money by playing "store."

Give your child small amounts of money to purchase items when you go shopping. Encourage your child to count their change after each transaction.

Encourage your child to create other combinations of money for the same amount. For example, ten cents can be made with one dime, two nickels, ten pennies or one nickel and five pennies.

Number Recognition

Have your child read the numbers on the license plates of other vehicles as you drive around town. This will not only reinforce number recognition but letter recognition as well!

Safety Tip: Make sure your child knows their address. Have your child write their address (with your assistance) and keep it with them:

> My Child
> 12345 Oak Street
> Any City, Any State 12345

Help your child memorize their phone number as well. Have them practice writing it and dialing it on the phone.

Number Words

Play hopscotch with your child. Instead of using numbers, write the number words in each hopscotch grid.

Patterns

Patterns can also be made from beads, blocks, paper clips, pencils and any other small objects, either alone or combined (blue block, red block, blue block, red block . . . pencil, paper clip, paper clip, pencil . . .). Begin a pattern with objects and have your child continue the pattern.

Place Value (Tens and Ones)

Rubber band or glue ten toothpicks together to represent "tens" and let your child practice counting by tens.

Let your child practice "trading" with pennies, dimes and a dollar to reinforce the concept of ones, tens and hundreds. Roll a die and let your child take as many pennies from the "pot" as the die indicates. When they have ten pennies, they can trade them in for a dime. Continue playing and trading pennies for dimes. When your child gets ten dimes, they can trade them in for a dollar!

Predicting

When reading a story to your child, pause often and ask, "What do you think will happen next?" This can also be done with videotapes.

You can also help your child practice predicting by giving clues about where you are going. For example, you might say that you are going to visit someone who lives in a white house. If your child needs more information, give additional clues.

Rhyming Words

Read familiar nursery rhymes to your child, and leave out the last line.
For example:

> Jack and Jill
> Went up the _____ .

Same and Different, Similarities, Opposites

Play a game with your child by giving him/her a clue, such as, "Can you bring me something that looks like a book?" or "Can you find a shirt that is the opposite of white?"

In the car, you can play "I Spy." Take turns with your child finding things that are opposite or similar, then give your child a clue such as, "I spy a sign that is the opposite of go." Have your child guess the object.

Give your child two similar objects such as a baseball and a balloon. Ask them to tell you ways the two are alike and ways they are different. Do the same with objects that are not very much alike, such as a ball and a toy truck. Again, ask your child to tell you how they are alike and different.

Sequencing

A daily activity like setting the table can help your child practice sequencing. Develop an order in which objects should be put on the table. You can also have your child put away toys according to size, such as from smallest to largest. Words could be put into alphabetical order.

After reading a story, ask your child to retell the story in their own words. Listen to see if they order the events correctly. If not, relate an event in the story and ask your child to tell you what happened next.

Talk to your child about order and sequencing in everyday life. Make lists together.

Example: 1. Go to the bank.
2. Go to the grocery store.

Shapes

Encourage your child to look at the different shapes of traffic signs and road signs. What shapes does your child see?

Shapes are part of our everyday lives. What shapes does your child see in their home, yard, etc.? List the shapes and objects. Add more as you find them.

Purchase or make a geoboard. To make a geoboard, pound sixteen 2-inch nails an equal distance apart into a 1-inch thick piece of wood. Pull rubber bands over the nails to create various geometric shapes. Talk with your child about the shapes they have created.

When going for a walk, have your child look around for shapes in the environment. For example, the front of a house might be a square, etc. Suggest a shape for your child to find.

Cut a long piece of yarn or string for your child. They can use it to make shapes. Draw a shape on a sheet of paper and have your child put the yarn on top of it to trace it. Then, have them make the shape without tracing it first. Do this with other shapes.

Spelling

Purchase magnetic alphabet letters and let your child practice spelling words and reading them to you. You can spell a word for your child, leaving out the vowel, as in "c _ t." Have your child add a vowel to complete the word.

Have your child write words on an index card with a black marker. Using a different colored crayon or marker to write the word again, have him/her "shadow" the first spelling. Let your child repeat this using several colors to create a "rainbow" effect.

Have your child spell words with alphabet soup letters, alphabet cereal letters or alphabet pasta letters.

Let your child spell words with bread dough letters. To make bread dough, help your child mix together the ingredients listed below.

$3\frac{3}{4}$ cups whole wheat flour

2 cups buttermilk

$\frac{1}{4}$ cup wheat germ

2 teaspoons baking soda

1 cup molasses

1 cup raisins

On wax paper, have your child roll out each piece of dough like a snake. Then, help them form each piece into a letter of the alphabet. Place the letters on a greased cookie sheet and bake at 350 degrees for 20 minutes or until golden brown.

Story Order

Encourage your child to tell you about their day. Write each event of your child's day on a separate strip of paper as they relate them to you. Then, cut the strips apart, and challenge them to rearrange the events in the correct order.

Tracking

To practice tracking, your child can make a road out of blocks, cardboard or paper. Then, they can "drive" a toy car on the road.

If your child has a bike or tricycle, you can set up a course for him/her to follow. This could also be done on in-line skates or a skateboard. They can practice tracking by following a jogging path. Mazes also provide practice in tracking. Provide a city map or draw one of your own. Point out where you are and where you are going. Let your child help find the shortest route to follow.

Writing

Fold a sheet of construction paper into a large cube-shaped block. Before folding, write a word on each side of the cube. Have your child throw the block, read the word that is faceup and write a sentence using the word.

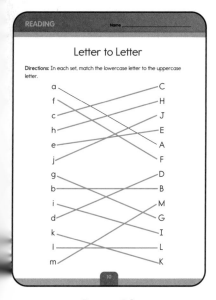

Page 10

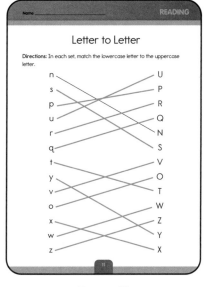

Page 11

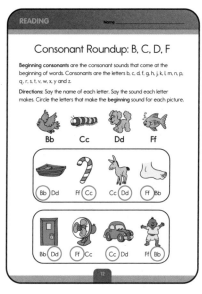

Page 12

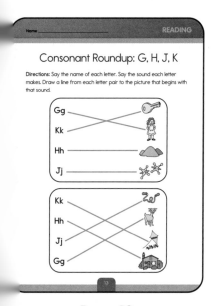

Page 13

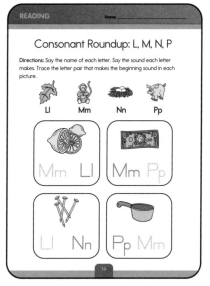

Page 14

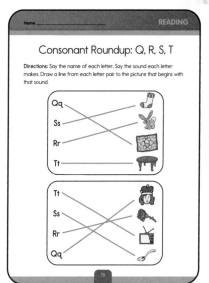

Page 15

ANSWER KEY

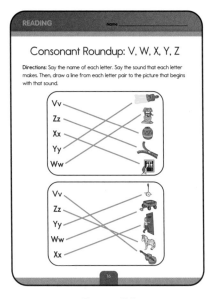

Page 16

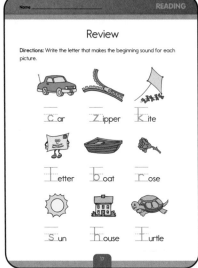

Page 17

Page 18

Page 19

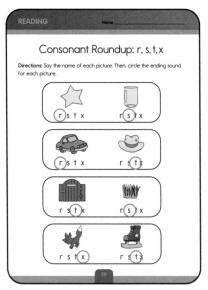

Page 20

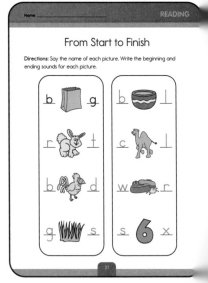

Page 21

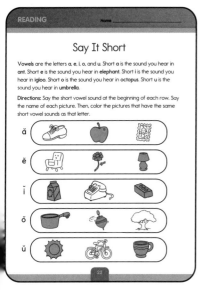

Page 22

Page 23

Page 24

Page 25

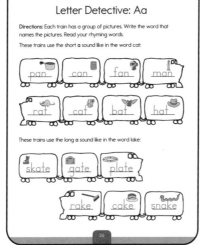

Page 26

Page 27

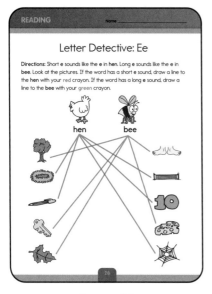

Page 28

Page 29

Page 30

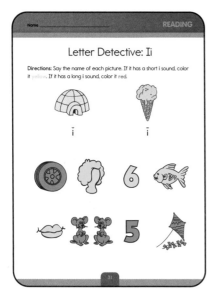

Page 31

Page 32

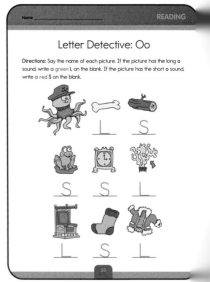

Page 33

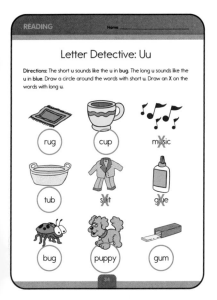

Page 34

Page 35

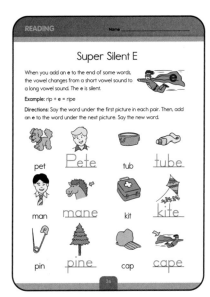

Page 36

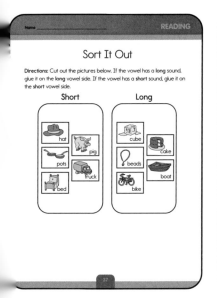

Page 37

Page 39

Page 41

ANSWER KEY

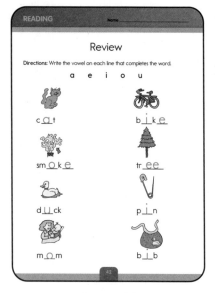

Page 42

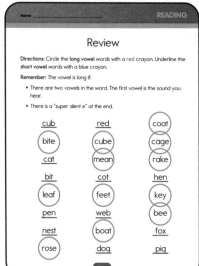

Page 43

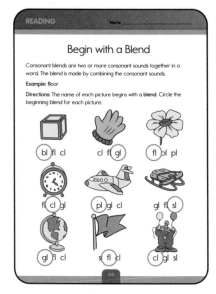

Page 44

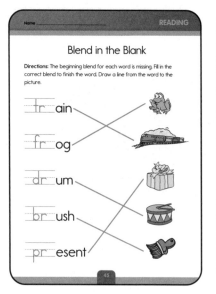

Page 45

Page 46

Page 47

Page 48

Page 49

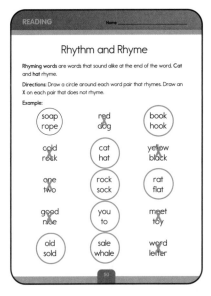

Page 50

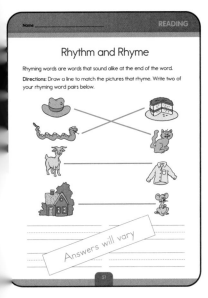

Page 51

Page 52

Page 53

Page 54

READING   Name _____

Two Words in One

Compound words are two words that are put together to make one new word.

Directions: Look at the pictures and the two words that are next to each other. Put the words together to make a new word. Write the new word.

Example:

house + boat = **houseboat**

side + walk = sidewalk

lip + stick = lipstick

sand + box = sandbox

lunch + box = lunchbox

Page 55

READING   Name _____

Double the Fun

Directions: Cut out the cards below. Turn them over. Take turns trying to make compound words. When a compound word is made, the player gets to keep the word.

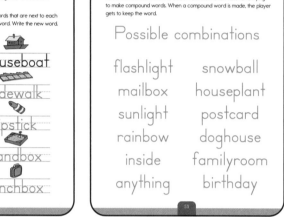

Possible combinations

flashlight	snowball
mailbox	houseplant
sunlight	postcard
rainbow	doghouse
inside	familyroom
anything	birthday

Page 57

READING   Name _____

The Name Game

You are a special person. Your name begins with a capital letter. We put a capital letter at the beginning of people's names because they are special.

Directions: Write your name. _____ pital letter?

Answers will vary

Directions: Write each person's name. Use a capital letter at the beginning.

Ted — Ted

Katie — Katie

Marcos — Marcos

Tim — Tim

Write a friend's name. Use a capital l...

Answers will vary

Page 58

READING   Name _____

7 Delightful Days

The days of the week begin with capital letters.

Directions: Write the days of the week in the spaces below. Put them in order. Be sure to start with capital letters.

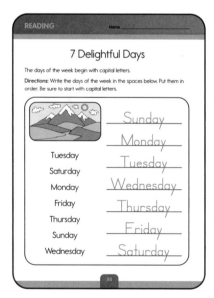

Sunday
Monday
Tuesday — Tuesday
Saturday
Monday — Wednesday
Friday
Thursday — Thursday
Thursday
Sunday — Friday
Wednesday — Saturday

Page 59

READING   Name _____

12 Marvelous Months

The months of the year begin with capital letters.

Directions: Write the months of the year in order on the calendar below. Be sure to use capital letters.

| January | July | June | April | November | February |
| October | December | March | September | May | August |

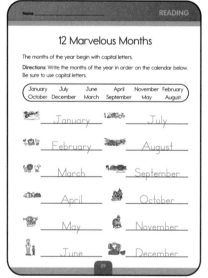

January — July
February — August
March — September
April — October
May — November
June — December

Page 60

READING   Name _____

Little Riddles

Directions: Read the word and write it on the line. Then, read each riddle and draw a line to the picture and word that tells about it.

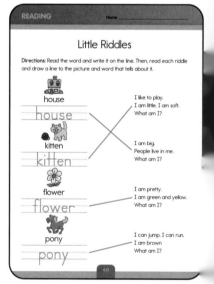

house — house

kitten — kitten

flower — flower

pony — pony

I like to play.
I am little. I am soft.
What am I?

I am big.
People live in me.
What am I?

I am pretty.
I am green and yellow.
What am I?

I can jump. I can run.
I am brown
What am I?

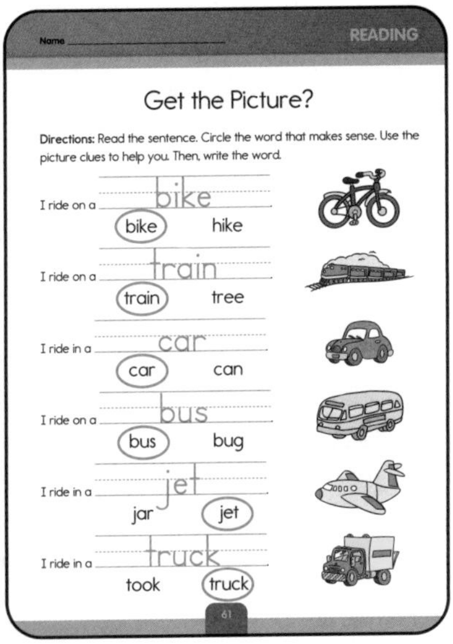

Name ______ READING

Get the Picture?

Directions: Read the sentence. Circle the word that makes sense. Use the picture clues to help you. Then, write the word.

I ride on a bike.
bike hike

I ride on a train.
train tree

I ride in a car.
car can

I ride on a bus.
bus bug

I ride in a jet.
jar jet

I ride in a truck.
took truck

61

Page 61

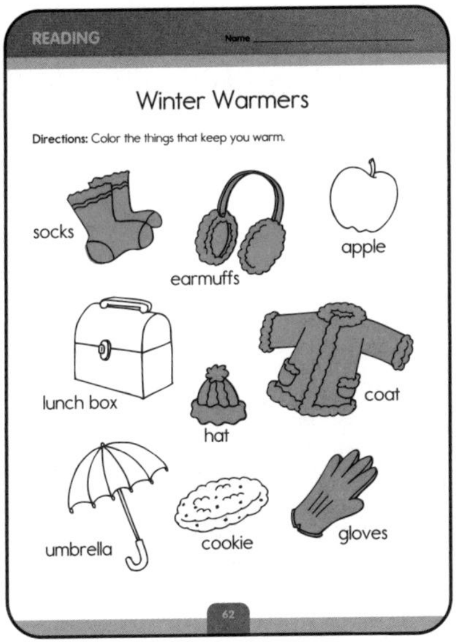

READING Name ______

Winter Warmers

Directions: Color the things that keep you warm.

62

Page 62

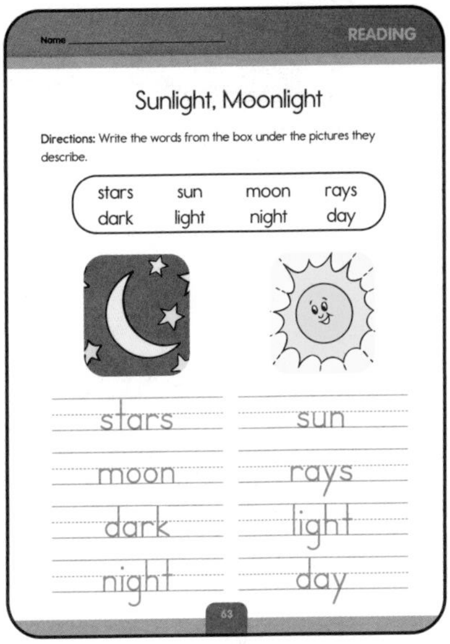

Name ______ READING

Sunlight, Moonlight

Directions: Write the words from the box under the pictures they describe.

stars sun moon rays
dark light night day

stars | sun
moon | rays
dark | light
night | day

63

Page 63

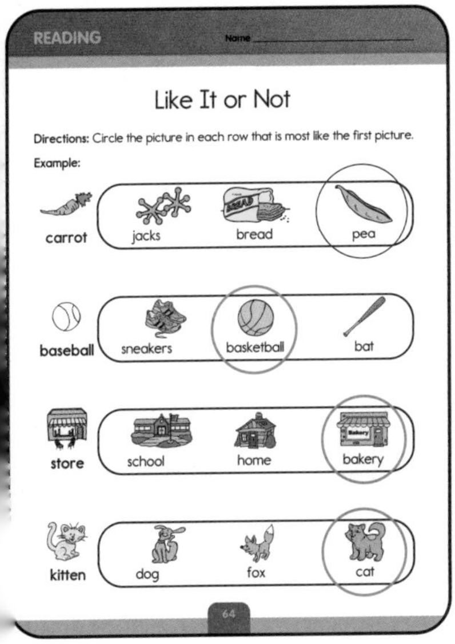

READING Name ______

Like It or Not

Directions: Circle the picture in each row that is most like the first picture.

Example:

carrot: jacks, bread, pea

baseball: sneakers, basketball, bat

store: school, home, bakery

kitten: dog, fox, cat

64

Page 64

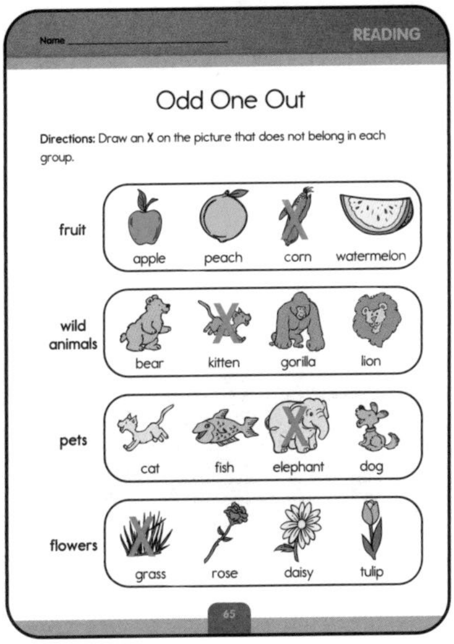

Name ______ READING

Odd One Out

Directions: Draw an X on the picture that does not belong in each group.

fruit: apple, peach, corn, watermelon

wild animals: bear, kitten, gorilla, lion

pets: cat, fish, elephant, dog

flowers: grass, rose, daisy, tulip

65

Page 65

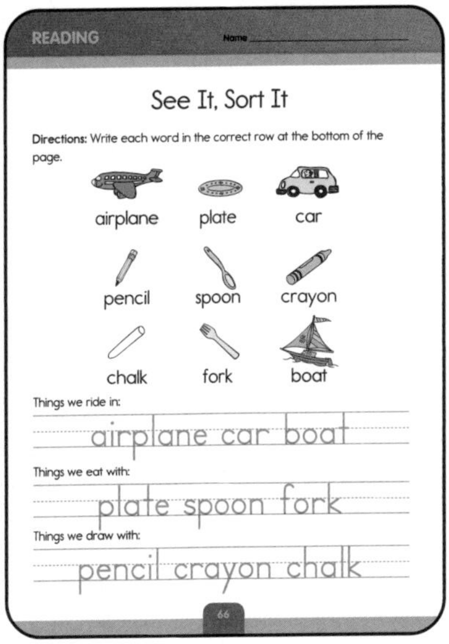

READING Name ______

See It, Sort It

Directions: Write each word in the correct row at the bottom of the page.

airplane plate car
pencil spoon crayon
chalk fork boat

Things we ride in: airplane car boat

Things we eat with: plate spoon fork

Things we draw with: pencil crayon chalk

66

Page 66

ANSWER KEY

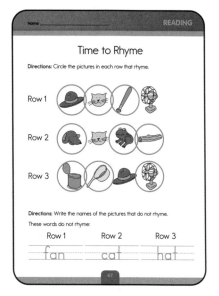

Time to Rhyme

Directions: Circle the pictures in each row that rhyme.

Row 1

Row 2

Row 3

Directions: Write the names of the pictures that do not rhyme.

These words do not rhyme:

Row 1 Row 2 Row 3

fan   cat   hat

Page 67

Twice the Fun!

Directions: Read the story. Then, use the words in the box and the picture to write your answers.

Ben and Ann are twin babies. They were born at the same time. They have the same mother. Ben is a boy baby. Ann is a girl baby.

mother	girl
bow	hat
boy	twins

1. Tell one way Ann and Ben are the same.

Answers may include: born at the same time or same mother

2. Ann and Ben are ___twins___

3. Tell two ways Ann and Ben are different.

Ann is a ___girl___ Ben is a ___boy___

Ann is wearing a ___bow___

Ben is wearing a ___hat___

Page 68

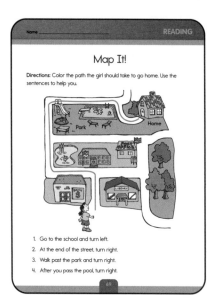

Map It!

Directions: Color the path the girl should take to go home. Use the sentences to help you.

1. Go to the school and turn left.
2. At the end of the street, turn right.
3. Walk past the park and turn right.
4. After you pass the pool, turn right.

Page 69

Make a Snowman!

Directions: Write the number of the sentence that goes with each picture in the circle.

1. Roll a large snowball for the snowman's bottom.
2. Make another snowball and put it on top of the first.
3. Put the last snowball on top.
4. Dress the snowman.

Page 70

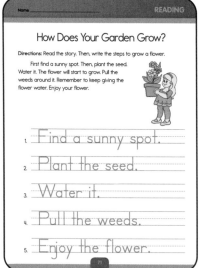

How Does Your Garden Grow?

Directions: Read the story. Then, write the steps to grow a flower.

First find a sunny spot. Then, plant the seed. Water it. The flower will start to grow. Pull the weeds around it. Remember to keep giving the flower water. Enjoy your flower.

1. Find a sunny spot.
2. Plant the seed.
3. Water it.
4. Pull the weeds.
5. Enjoy the flower.

Page 71

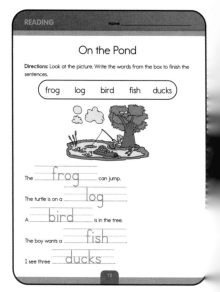

On the Pond

Directions: Look at the picture. Write the words from the box to finish the sentences.

| frog | log | bird | fish | ducks |

The ___frog___ can jump.

The turtle is on a ___log___

A ___bird___ is in the tree.

The boy wants a ___fish___

I see three ___ducks___

Page 72

An Apple a Day

Directions: Read about apples. Then, write the answers.

I like ___ . Do you?

Some ___ are red.

Some ___ are green.

Some ___ are yellow.

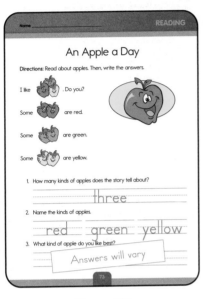

1. How many kinds of apples does the story tell about?

three

2. Name the kinds of apples.

red   green   yellow

3. What kind of apple do you like best?

Answers will vary

Page 73

Puddle Jumping

Directions: Read the story. Write the words from the story that complete each sentence.

Jada and Bill like to play in the rain. They take off their shoes and socks. They splash in the puddles. It feels cold! It is fun to splash!

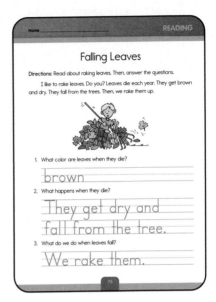

Jada and Bill like to **play in the rain**

They take off their **shoes and socks**

They splash in **the puddles**

Do you like to splash in puddles? (Yes)   No

Page 74

Falling Leaves

Directions: Read about raking leaves. Then, answer the questions.

I like to rake leaves. Do you? Leaves die each year. They get brown and dry. They fall from the trees. Then, we rake them up.

1. What color are leaves when they die?

brown

2. What happens when they die?

They get dry and fall from the tree.

3. What do we do when leaves fall?

We rake them.

Page 75

Bunches of Balloons

Directions: Read the story. Then, answer the questions.

Some balloons float. They are filled with gas. Some do not float. They are filled with air. Some clowns carry balloons. Balloons come in many colors. What color do you like?

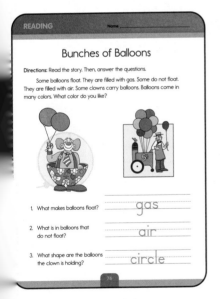

1. What makes balloons float?   **gas**

2. What is in balloons that do not float?   **air**

3. What shape are the balloons the clown is holding?   **circle**

Page 76

Time to Party!

Directions: Read about the party. Then, complete the invitation.

The party will be at Dog's house. The party will start at 1:00 P.M. It will last 2 hours. Write your birthday for the date of the party.

Party Invitation

Where: **Dog's house**

Answers will vary

Time It Begins: **1:00** P.M.

Time It Ends: **3:00** P.M.

Answers will vary

Directions: On the last line, write something else about the party.

Page 77

Review

Directions: Read the story. Then, circle the pictures of things that are wet.

Some things used in baking are dry. Some things used in baking are wet. To bake a cake, first mix the salt, sugar and flour. Then, add the egg. Now, add the milk. Stir. Put the cake in the oven.

Directions: Tell the order to mix things when you bake a cake.

1. **salt**
2. **sugar**
3. **flour**
4. **egg**
5. **milk**

Directions: Circle the answers.

6. The first things to mix are   (dry)   wet.

7. Where are cakes baked?   (oven)   grill

Page 78

Page 79

A Tiger Tale

Directions: Read about tigers. Then, write the answers.

Tigers sleep during the day. They hunt at night. Tigers eat meat. They hunt deer. They like to eat wild pigs. If they cannot find meat, tigers will eat fish.

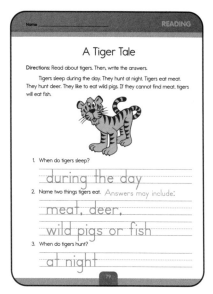

1. When do tigers sleep?

   during the day

2. Name two things tigers eat. *Answers may include:*

   meat, deer,
   wild pigs or fish

3. When do tigers hunt?

   at night

Page 79

Page 80

Get a Clue

Directions: Read the story about tigers again. Then, complete the puzzle.

```
¹F I S H
    L
  ³M E A T
    E
  ⁴P I G
```

Across

1. When tigers cannot get meat, they eat _____.
3. The food tigers like best is _____.
4. Tigers like to eat this meat: wild _____.

Down

2. Tigers do this during the day.

Page 80

Page 81

Tiger Art

Directions: Follow directions to complete the picture of the tiger.

1. Draw **black** stripes on the tiger's body and tail.
2. Color the tiger's tongue red.
3. Draw claws on the feet.
4. Draw a **black** nose and two **black** eyes on the tiger's face.
5. Color the rest of the tiger orange.
6. Draw tall, green grass for the tiger to sleep in.

Page 81

Page 82

Simon Says

Directions: Read how to play Simon Says. Then, answer the questions.

Simon Says

Here is how to play Simon Says: One kid is Simon. Simon is the leader. Everyone must do what Simon says and does but only if the leader says, "Simon says" first. Let's try it. "Simon says, 'Pat your head.'" "Simon says, 'Pat your nose. Pat your toes.'" Oops! Did you pat your toes? I did not say, "Simon says," first. If you patted your toes, you are out!

Simon says, CLAP YOUR HANDS!

1. Who is the leader in this game?

   Simon

2. What must the leader say first each time?

   "Simon says"

3. What happens if you do something and the leader did not say, "Simon says"?

   You are out.

Page 82

Page 83

Eyes on Simon

Directions: Read each sentence. Look at the picture next to it. Circle the picture if the person is playing Simon Says correctly.

1. Simon says, "Put your hands on your hips."
2. Simon says, "Stand on one leg."
3. Simon says, "Put your hands on your head."
4. Simon says, "Ride a bike."
5. Simon says, "Jump up and down."
6. Simon says, "Pet a dog."

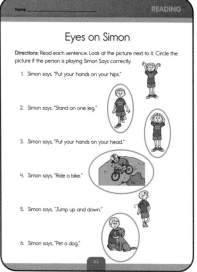

Page 83

Page 84

A Message from Simon

Directions: Read the sentences. If Simon tells you to do something, follow the directions. If Simon does not tell you to do something, go to the next sentence.

1. Simon says: Cross out all the numbers 2 through 9.
2. Simon says: Cross out the vowel that is in the word "sun."
3. Cross out the letter "B."
4. Cross out the vowels "A" and "E."
5. Simon says: Cross out the consonants in the word "cup."
6. Cross out the letter "Z."
7. Simon says: Cross out all the "K's."
8. Simon says: Read your message.

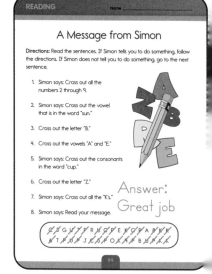

Answer:
Great job

C̶2̶G̶U̶7̶P̶R̶U̶G̶R̶E̶K̶O̶R̶A̶B̶V̶K̶
N̶T̶R̶U̶P̶J̶E̶5̶P̶O̶K̶A̶P̶B̶U̶R̶A̶X̶

Page 84

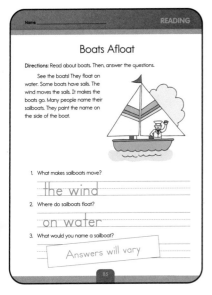

Page 85

Page 86

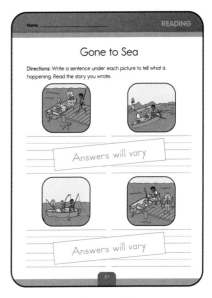

Page 87

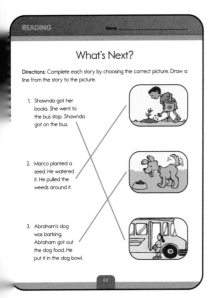

Page 88

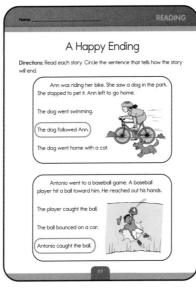

Page 89

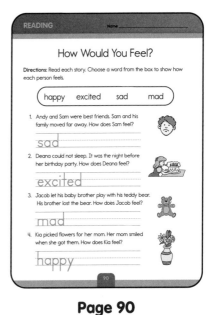

Page 90

ANSWER KEY

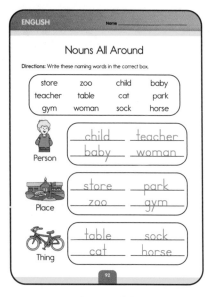

Page 92

Page 93

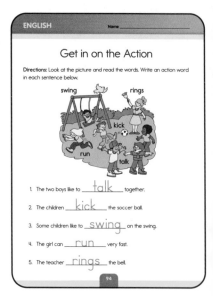

Page 94

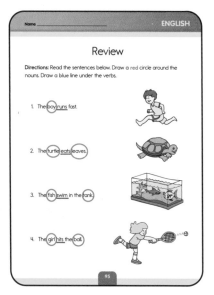

Page 95

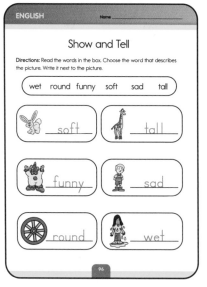

Page 96

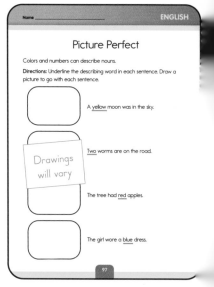

Page 97

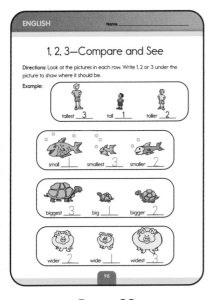

Page 98

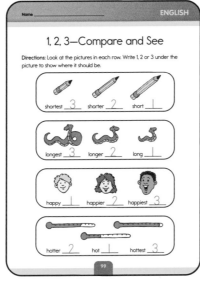

Page 99

Page 100

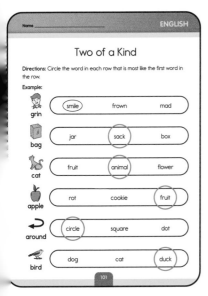

Page 101

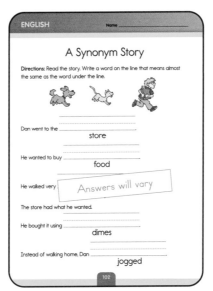

Page 102

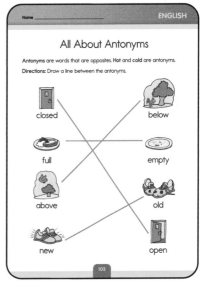

Page 103

Page 104

Opposites Attract

Directions: Circle the picture in each row that is the opposite of the first picture.

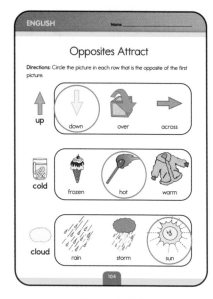

Page 104

Page 105

Fishing for Antonyms

Directions: Read each clue. Write the answers in the puzzle.

high   yes   left
heavy   tight
safe   full

Across:
1. Opposite of low
2. Opposite of no
4. Opposite of empty
6. Opposite of loose

Down:
1. Opposite of light
3. Opposite of dangerous
5. Opposite of right

Page 105

Page 106

Sound Alikes

Homophones are words that **sound** the same but are spelled differently and mean something different. **Blew** and **blue** are homophones.

Directions: Look at the word pairs. Choose the word that describes the picture. Write the word on the line next to the picture.

1. sew   so   sew
2. pair   pear   pear
3. eye   I   eye
4. see   sea   sea

Page 106

Page 107

Sound Alikes

Directions: Read each sentence. Underline the two words that sound the same but are spelled differently and mean something different.

1. Tom <u>ate</u> <u>eight</u> grapes.
2. Becky <u>read</u> Little <u>Red</u> Riding Hood.
3. I went <u>to</u> buy <u>two</u> dolls.
4. Five blue feathers <u>blew</u> in the wind.
5. Would you get <u>wood</u> for the fire?

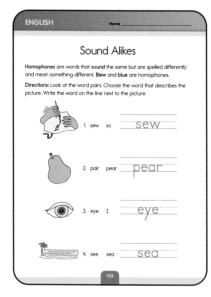

Page 107

Page 108

Say it with a Sentence

Sentences begin with capital letters.

Directions: Read the sentences and write them below. Begin each sentence with a capital letter.

Example:

the cat is fat.
The cat is fat.

my dog is big.
My dog is big.

the boy is sad.
The boy is sad.

bikes are fun!
Bikes are fun!

dad can bake.
Dad can bake.

Page 108

Page 109

All in Order

If you change the order of the words in a sentence, you can change the meaning of a sentence.

Directions: Read the sentences. Draw a circle around the sentence that describes the picture.

Example:
(The fox jumped over the dogs.)
The dogs jumped over the fox.

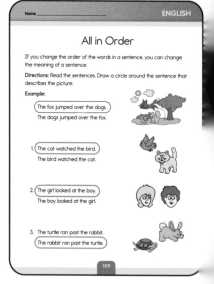

1. (The cat watched the bird.)
The bird watched the cat.

2. (The girl looked at the boy.)
The boy looked at the girl.

3. The turtle ran past the rabbit.
(The rabbit ran past the turtle.)

Page 109

Page 110

ENGLISH   Name _____

Lemonade for Sale!

Directions: Look at the picture. Put the words in order. Write the sentences on the lines below.

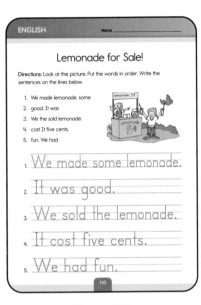

1. We made lemonade. some
2. good. It was
3. We the sold lemonade.
4. cost It five cents.
5. fun. We had

1. We made some lemonade.
2. It was good.
3. We sold the lemonade.
4. It cost five cents.
5. We had fun.

110

Page 110

Page 111

Name _____   **ENGLISH**

Telling Sentences: Pet Crazy

Directions: Read the sentences and write them below. Begin each sentence with a capital letter. End each sentence with a period.

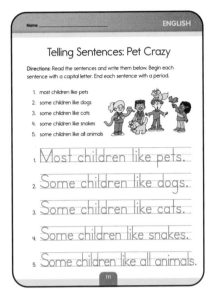

1. most children like pets
2. some children like dogs
3. some children like cats
4. some children like snakes
5. some children like all animals

1. Most children like pets.
2. Some children like dogs.
3. Some children like cats.
4. Some children like snakes.
5. Some children like all animals.

111

Page 111

Page 112

ENGLISH   Name _____

Telling Sentences: Going Shopping

Directions: Read the sentences and write them below. Begin each sentence with a capital letter. End each sentence with a period.

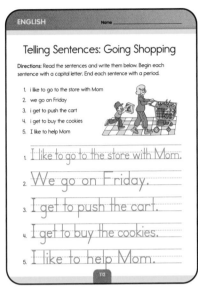

1. i like to go to the store with Mom
2. we go on Friday
3. i get to push the cart
4. i get to buy the cookies
5. I like to help Mom

1. I like to go to the store with Mom.
2. We go on Friday.
3. I get to push the cart.
4. I get to buy the cookies.
5. I like to help Mom.

112

Page 112

Page 113

Name _____   **ENGLISH**

Asking Sentences: Monkeying Around

Directions: Write the first word of each asking sentence. Be sure to begin each question with a capital letter. End each question with a question mark.

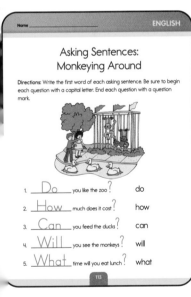

1. __Do__ you like the zoo?   do
2. __How__ much does it cost?   how
3. __Can__ you feed the ducks?   can
4. __Will__ you see the monkeys?   will
5. __What__ time will you eat lunch?   what

113

Page 113

Page 114

ENGLISH   Name _____

Asking Sentences: Getting to Know You

Directions: Read the asking sentences. Write the sentences below. Begin each sentence with a capital letter. End each sentence with a question mark.

1. what game will we play
2. do you like to read
3. how old are you
4. who is your best friend
5. can you tie your shoes

1. What game will we play?
2. Do you like to read?
3. How old are you?
4. Who is your best friend?
5. Can you tie your shoes?

114

Page 114

Page 115

Name _____   **ENGLISH**

Punctuation Parade

Directions: Put a period or a question mark at the end of each sentence below.

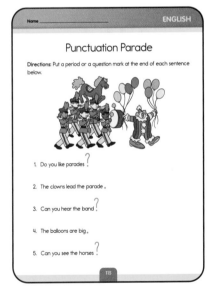

1. Do you like parades?
2. The clowns lead the parade.
3. Can you hear the band?
4. The balloons are big.
5. Can you see the horses?

115

Page 115

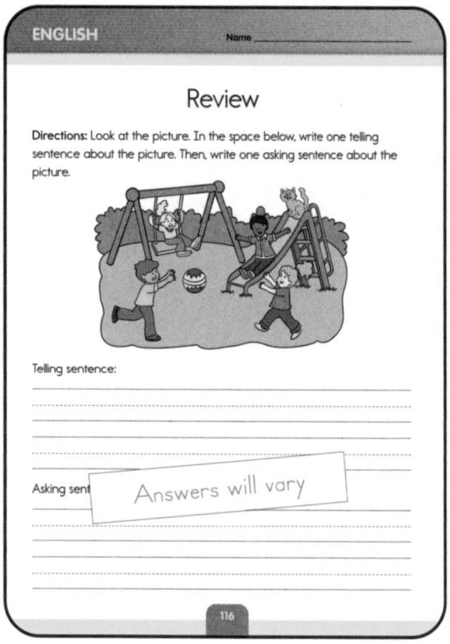
ENGLISH Name

Review

Directions: Look at the picture. In the space below, write one telling sentence about the picture. Then, write one asking sentence about the picture.

Telling sentence:

Asking sent

Answers will vary

116

Page 116

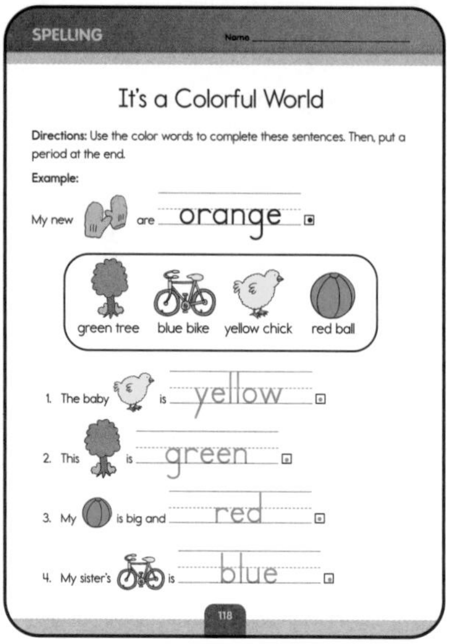
SPELLING Name

It's a Colorful World

Directions: Use the color words to complete these sentences. Then, put a period at the end.

Example:

My new are orange.

green tree blue bike yellow chick red ball

1. The baby is yellow.
2. This is green.
3. My is big and red.
4. My sister's is blue.

118

Page 118

Name SPELLING

Finish the Pictures

Directions: Read the words. Finish the pictures.

a red ball

a black hat

a yellow sun

a pink kite

an orange balloon

a blue umbrella

119

Page 119

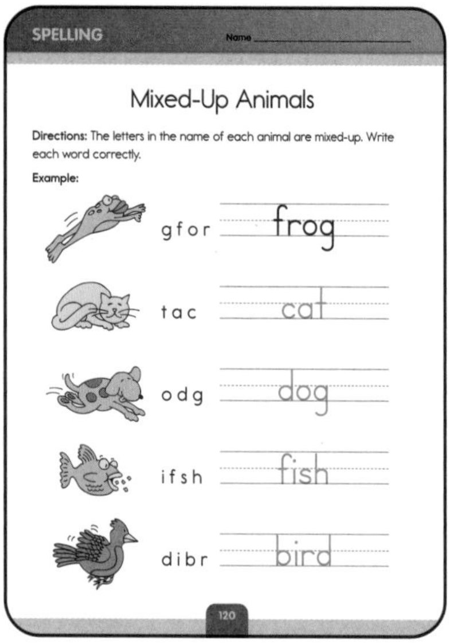
SPELLING Name

Mixed-Up Animals

Directions: The letters in the name of each animal are mixed-up. Write each word correctly.

Example:

gfor frog

tac cat

odg dog

ifsh fish

dibr bird

120

Page 120

Name SPELLING

Busy, Busy Animals

Directions: Use the words in the pictures to write a sentence about each animal. Put a period at the end of each sentence.

Example:

The eats bugs.

The frog eats bugs.

The drinks milk

The cat drinks milk.

The eats seeds

The bird eats seeds.

The jumps out

The dog jumps out.

The meet

The fish meet.

121

Page 121

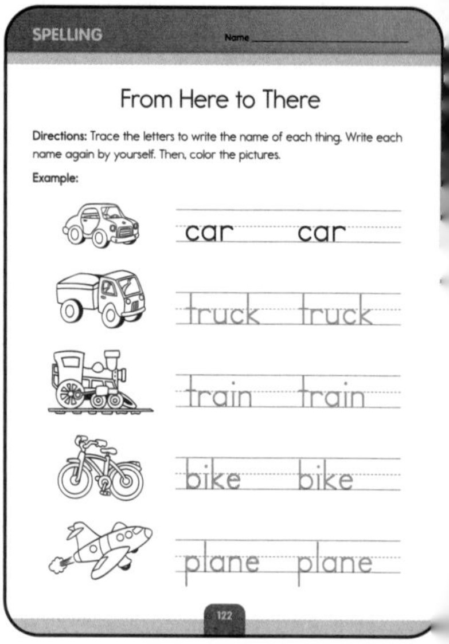
SPELLING Name

From Here to There

Directions: Trace the letters to write the name of each thing. Write each name again by yourself. Then, color the pictures.

Example:

car car

truck truck

train train

bike bike

plane plane

122

Page 122

Page 123

Page 124

Page 125

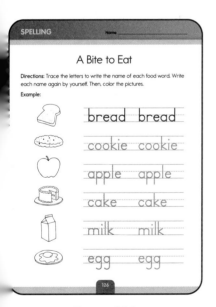

Page 126

Page 127

Page 128

Page 129

Page 130

Page 131

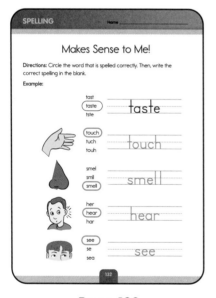

Page 132

Page 133

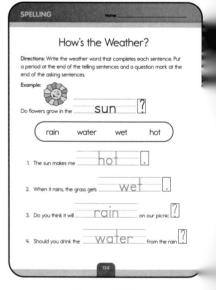

Page 134

Page 135

Page 136

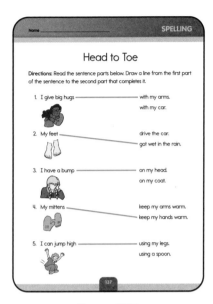

Page 137

Page 138

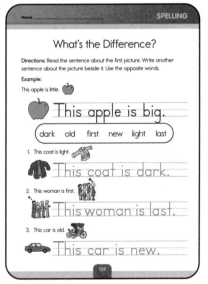

Page 139

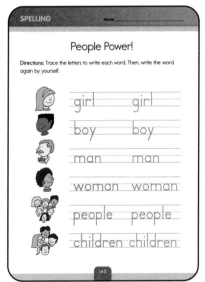

Page 140

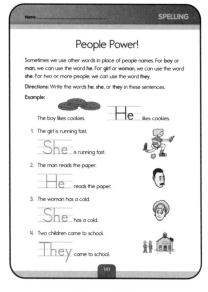

Page 141

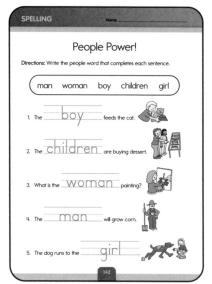

Page 142

Page 144

Page 145

Page 146

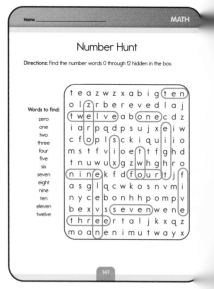

Page 147

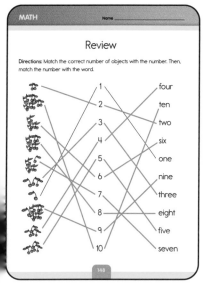

Page 148

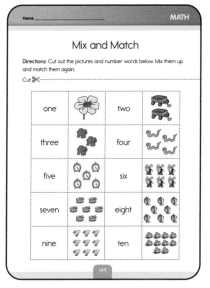

Page 149

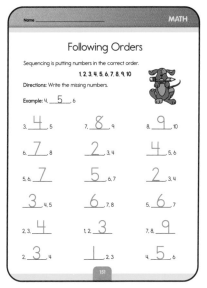

Page 151

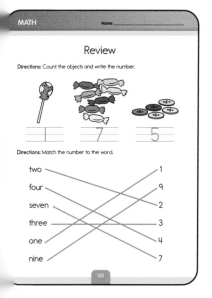

Page 152

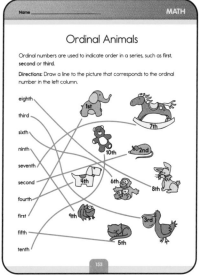

Page 153

Page 154

Page 155

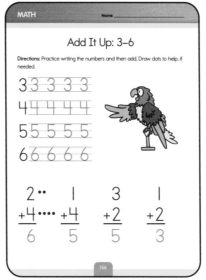

Page 156

Page 157

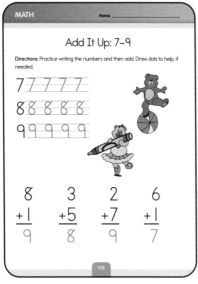

Page 158

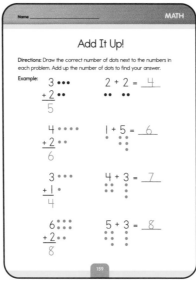

Page 159

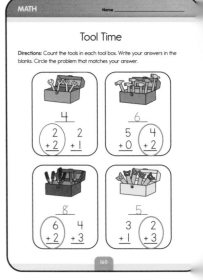

Page 160

Page 161

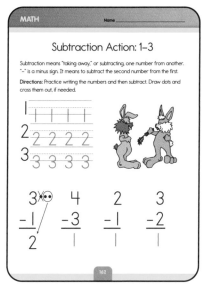

Page 162

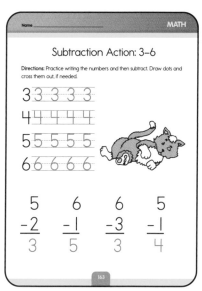

Page 163

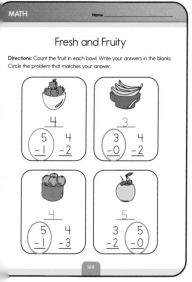

Page 164

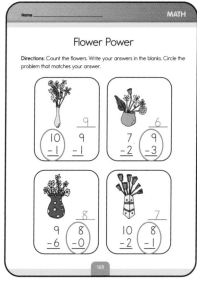

Page 165

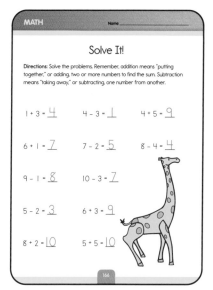

Page 166

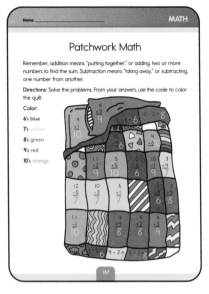

Page 167

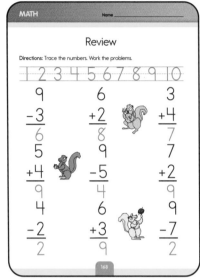

Page 168

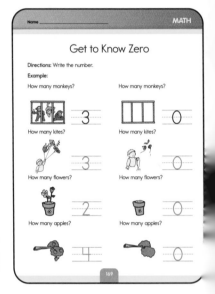

Page 169

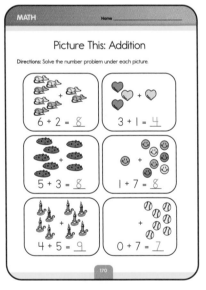

Page 170

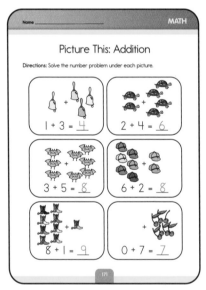

Page 171

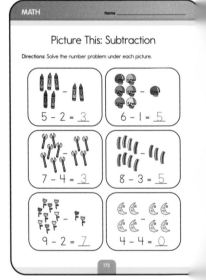

Page 172

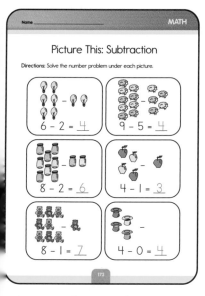

Page 173

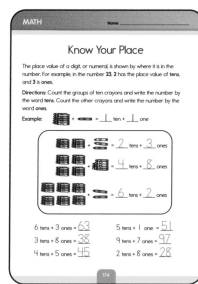

Page 174

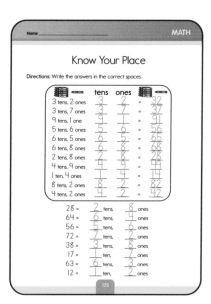

Page 175

Page 176

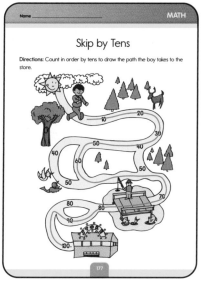

Page 177

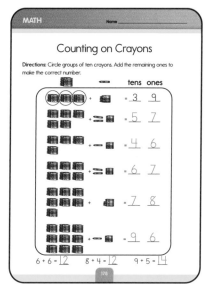

Page 178

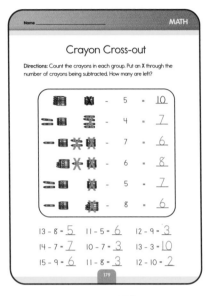

Page 179

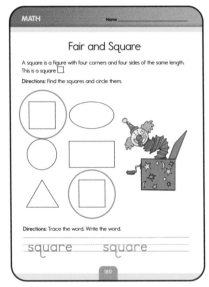

Page 180

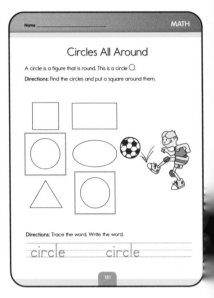

Page 181

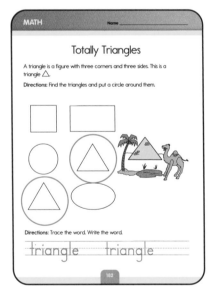

Page 182

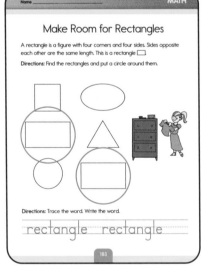

Page 183

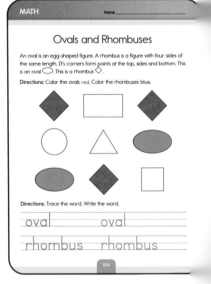

Page 184

Page 185

Page 186

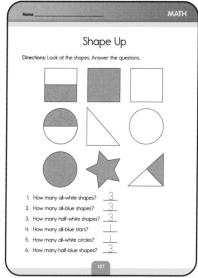

Page 187

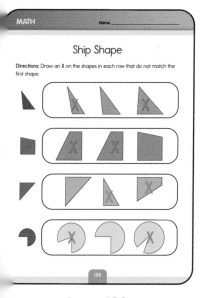

Page 188

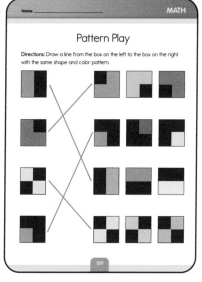

Page 189

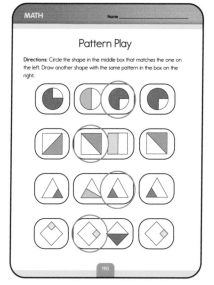

Page 190

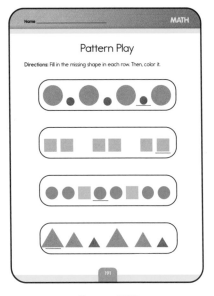

Page 191

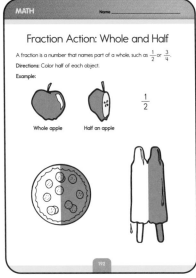

Page 192

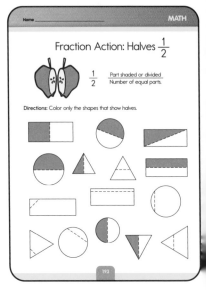

Page 193

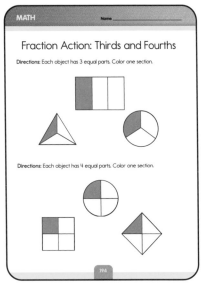

Page 194

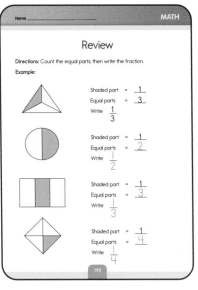

Page 195

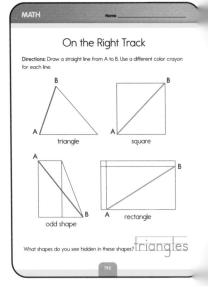

Page 196

Page 197

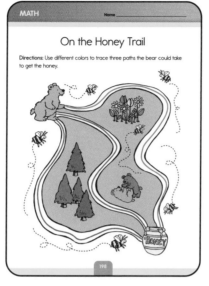

Page 198

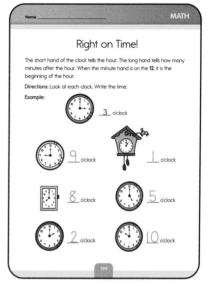

Page 199

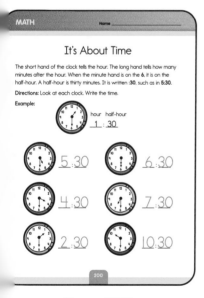

Page 200

Page 201

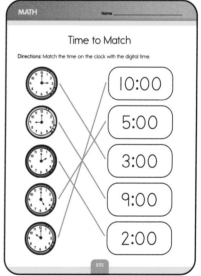

Page 202

ANSWER KEY

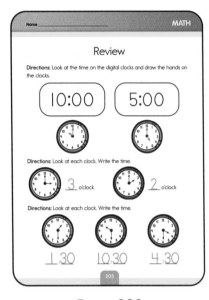

Page 203

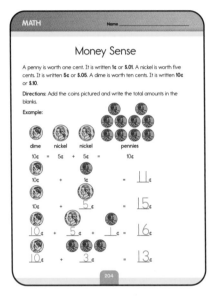

Page 204

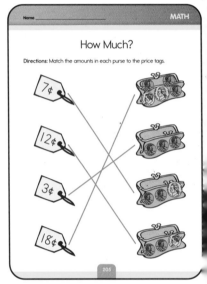

Page 205

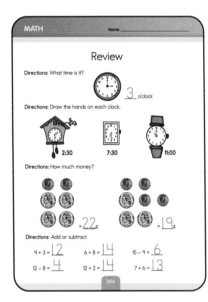

Page 206

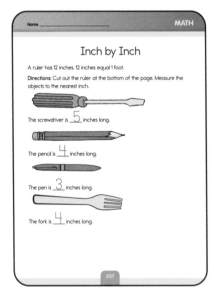

Page 207

JUST SO STORIES

RUDYARD

JUST SO

ILLUSTRATED

KIPLING
STORIES

by Nicolas

Doubleday

NEW YORK LONDON TORONTO SYDNEY AUCKLAND

PUBLISHED BY DOUBLEDAY, A DIVISION OF
BANTAM DOUBLEDAY DELL PUBLISHING GROUP, INC.
666 FIFTH AVENUE, NEW YORK, NEW YORK 10103

DOUBLEDAY AND THE PORTRAYAL OF AN ANCHOR WITH A DOLPHIN
ARE TRADEMARKS OF DOUBLEDAY, A DIVISION OF
BANTAM DOUBLEDAY DELL PUBLISHING GROUP, INC.

LIBRARY OF CONGRESS CATALOG CARD NUMBER 88-28986
C.I.P. DATA APPLIED FOR
ISBN 0-385-02129-1
ISBN 0-385-26133-0 (PBK.)

CONTENTS

HOW THE WHALE GOT HIS THROAT

IN the sea, once upon a time, O my Best Beloved, there was a Whale, and he ate fishes. He ate the starfish and the garfish, and the crab and the dab, and the plaice and the dace, and the skate and his mate, and the mackereel and the pickereel, and the really truly twirly-whirly eel. All the fishes he could find in all the sea he ate with his mouth—so! Till at last there was only one small fish left in all the sea, and he was a small 'Stute Fish, and he swam a little behind the Whale's right ear, so as to be out of harm's way. Then the Whale stood up on his tail and said, 'I'm hungry.' And the small 'Stute Fish said in a small 'stute voice, 'Noble and generous Cetacean, have you ever tasted Man?'

'No,' said the Whale. 'What is it like?'

'Nice,' said the small 'Stute Fish. 'Nice but nubbly.'

'Then fetch me some,' said the Whale, and he made the sea froth up with his tail.

'One at a time is enough,' said the 'Stute Fish. 'If you swim to latitude Fifty North, longitude Forty West (that is magic), you will find, sitting on a raft, in the middle of the sea, with nothing on but a pair of blue canvas breeches, a pair of suspenders (you must not forget the suspenders, Best Beloved), and a jack-knife, one shipwrecked Mariner, who, it is only fair to tell you, is a man of infinite-resource-and-sagacity.'

So the Whale swam and swam to latitude Fifty North, longitude Forty West, as fast as he could swim, and on a raft, in the middle of the sea, with nothing to wear except a pair of blue canvas breeches, a pair of suspenders (you must particularly remember the suspenders, Best Beloved), and a jack-knife, he found one single, solitary shipwrecked Mariner, trailing his toes in the water. (He had his mummy's leave to paddle, or else he would never have done it because he was a man of infinite-resource-and-sagacity.)

Then the Whale opened his mouth back and back and back till it nearly touched his tail, and he swallowed the shipwrecked Mariner, and the raft he was sitting on, and his blue canvas breeches, and the suspenders

(which you *must* not forget), *and* the jack-knife—He swallowed them all down into his warm, dark, inside cupboards, and then he smacked his lips—so, and turned round three times on his tail.

But as soon as the Mariner, who was a man of infinite-resource-and-sagacity, found himself truly inside the Whale's warm, dark, inside cupboards, he stumped and he jumped and he thumped and he bumped, and he pranced and he danced, and he banged and he clanged, and he hit and he bit, and he leaped and he creeped, and he prowled and he howled, and he hopped and he dropped, and he cried and he sighed, and he crawled and he bawled, and he stepped and he lepped, and he danced hornpipes where he shouldn't, and the Whale felt most unhappy indeed. (*Have* you forgotten the suspenders?)

10

So he said to the 'Stute Fish, 'This man is very nubbly, and besides he is making me hic-cough. What shall I do?'

'Tell him to come out,' said the 'Stute Fish.

So the Whale called down his own throat to the shipwrecked Mariner, 'Come out and behave yourself. I've got the hiccoughs.'

'Nay, nay!' said the Mariner. 'Not so, but far otherwise. Take me to my natal-shore and the white-cliffs-of-Albion, and I'll think about it.' And he began to dance more than ever.

'You had better take him home,' said the 'Stute Fish to the Whale. 'I ought to have warned you that he is a man of infinite-resource-and-sagacity.'

So the Whale swam and swam and swam, with both flippers and his tail, as hard as he could for the hiccoughs; and at last he saw the Mariner's natal-shore and the white-cliffs-of-Albion, and he rushed half-way up the beach, and opened his mouth wide and wide and wide, and said, 'Change here for Winchester,

Ashuelot, Nashua, Keene, and stations on the *Fitch*burg Road;' and just as he said 'Fitch' the Mariner walked out of his mouth. But while the Whale had been swimming, the Mariner, who was indeed a person of infinite-resource-and-sagacity, had taken his jack-knife and cut up the raft into a little square grating all running criss-cross, and he had tied it firm with his suspenders (*now* you know why you were not to forget the suspenders!), and he dragged that grating good and tight into the Whale's throat, and there it 'stuck! Then he recited the following *Sloka*, which, as you have not heard it, I will now proceed to relate—

> *By means of a grating*
> *I have stopped your ating.*

For the Mariner he was also an Hi-ber-ni-an. And he stepped out on the shingle, and went home to his mother, who had given him leave to trail his toes in the water; and he married and lived happily ever afterward. So did the Whale. But from that day on, the grating in his throat, which he could neither cough up nor swallow down, prevented him eating anything except very, very small fish; and that is the reason why whales nowadays never eat men or boys or little girls.

The small 'Stute Fish went and hid himself in the mud under the Door-sills of the Equator. He was afraid that the Whale might be angry with him.

The Sailor took the jack-knife home. He was wearing the blue canvas breeches when he walked out on the shingle. The suspenders were left behind, you see, to tie the grating with; and that is the end of *that* tale.

HOW THE CAMEL GOT HIS HUMP

NOW this is the next tale, and it tells how the Camel got his big hump.

In the beginning of years, when the world was so new and all, and the Animals were just beginning to work for Man, there was a Camel, and he lived in the middle of a Howling Desert because he did not want to work; and besides, he was a Howler himself. So he ate sticks and thorns and tamarisks and milkweed and prickles, most 'scruciating idle; and when anybody spoke to him he said 'Humph!' Just 'Humph!' and no more.

Presently the Horse came to him on Monday morning, with a saddle on his back and a bit in his mouth, and said, 'Camel, O Camel, come out and trot like the rest of us.'

'Humph!' said the Camel; and the Horse went away and told the Man.

Presently the Dog came to him, with a stick in his mouth, and said, 'Camel, O Camel, come and fetch and carry like the rest of us.'

'Humph!' said the Camel; and the Dog went away and told the Man.

Presently the Ox came to him, with the yoke on his neck and said, 'Camel, O Camel, come and plough like the rest of us.'

'Humph!' said the Camel; and the Ox went away and told the Man.

At the end of the day the Man called the Horse and the Dog and the Ox together, and said, 'Three, O Three, I'm very sorry for you (with the world so new-and-all); but that Humph-thing in the Desert can't work, or he would have been here by now, so I am going to leave him alone, and you must work double-time to make up for it.'

13

That made the Three very angry (with the world so new-and-all), and they held a palaver, and an *indaba,* and a *punchayet,* and a pow-wow on the edge of the Desert; and the Camel came chewing milkweed *most* 'scruciating idle, and laughed at them. Then he said 'Humph!' and went away again.

Presently there came along the Djinn in charge of All Deserts, rolling in a cloud of dust (Djinns always travel that way because it is Magic), and he stopped to palaver and pow-pow with the Three.

'Djinn of All Deserts,' said the Horse, '*is* it right for any one to be idle, with the world so new-and-all?'

'Certainly not,' said the Djinn.

'Well,' said the Horse, 'there's a thing in the middle of your Howling Desert (and he's a Howler himself) with a long neck and long legs, and he hasn't done a stroke of work since Monday morning. He won't trot.'

'Whew!' said the Djinn, whistling, 'that's my Camel, for all the gold in Arabia! What does he say about it?'

'He says "Humph!" ' said the Dog; 'and he won't fetch and carry.'

'Does he say anything else?'

'Only "Humph!"; and he won't plough,' said the Ox.

'Very good,' said the Djinn. 'I'll humph him if you will kindly wait a minute.'

The Djinn rolled himself up in his dust-cloak, and took a bearing across the desert, and found the Camel most 'scruciatingly idle, looking at his own reflection in a pool of water.

'My long and bubbling friend,' said the Djinn, 'what's this I hear of your doing no work, with the world so new-and-all?'

'Humph!' said the Camel.

The Djinn sat down, with his chin in his hand, and began to think a Great Magic, while the Camel looked at his own reflection in the pool of water.

'You've given the Three extra work ever since Monday morning, all on account of your 'scruciating idleness,' said the Djinn; and he went on thinking Magics, with his chin in his hand.

'Humph!' said the Camel.

'I shouldn't say that again if I were you,'

14

said the Djinn; 'you might say it once too often. Bubbles, I want you to work.'

And the Camel said 'Humph!' again; but no sooner had he said it than he saw his back, that he was so proud of, puffing up and puffing up into a great big lolloping humph.

'Do you see that?' said the Djinn. 'That's your very own humph that you've brought upon your very own self by not working. To-day is Thursday, and you've done no work since Monday, when the work began. Now you are going to work.'

'How can I,' said the Camel, 'with this humph on my back?'

'That's made a-purpose,' said the Djinn, 'all because you missed those three days. You will be able to work now for three days without eating, because you can live on your humph; and don't you ever say I never did anything for you. Come out of the Desert and go to the Three, and behave. Humph yourself!'

And the Camel humphed himself, humph and all, and went away to join the Three. And from that day to this the Camel always wears a humph (we call it 'hump' now, not to hurt his feelings); but he has never yet caught up with the three days that he missed at the beginning of the world, and he has never yet learned how to behave.

15

HOW THE RHINOCEROS GOT HIS SKIN

ONCE upon a time, on an uninhabited island on the shores of the Red Sea, there lived a Parsee from whose hat the rays of the sun were reflected in more-than-oriental splendour. And the Parsee lived by the Red Sea with nothing but his hat and his knife and a cooking-stove of the kind that you must particularly never touch. And one day he took flour and water and currants and plums and sugar and things, and made himself one cake which was two feet across and three feet thick. It was indeed a Superior Comestible (*that*'s magic), and he put it on the stove because *he* was allowed to cook on that stove, and he baked it and he baked it till it was all done brown and smelt most sentimental. But just as he was going to eat it there came down to the beach from the Altogether Uninhabited Interior one Rhinoceros with a horn on his nose, two piggy eyes, and few manners. In those days the Rhinoceros's skin fitted him quite tight. There were no wrinkles in it anywhere. He looked exactly like a Noah's Ark Rhinoceros, but of course much bigger. All the same, he had no manners then, and he has no manners now, and he never will have any manners. He said, 'How!' and the Parsee left that cake and climbed to the top of a palm tree with nothing on but his hat, from which the rays of the sun were always reflected in more-than-oriental splendour. And the Rhinoceros upset the oil-stove with his nose, and the cake rolled on the sand, and he spiked that cake on the horn of his nose, and he ate it, and he went away, waving his tail, to the desolate and Exclusively Uninhabited Interior which abuts on the islands of Mazanderan, Socotra, and the Promontories of the Larger Equinox. Then the Parsee came down from his palm-tree and put the stove on its legs and recited the following *Sloka,* which, as you have not heard, I will now proceed to relate:—

> *Them that takes cakes*
> *Which the Parsee-man bakes*
> *Makes dreadful mistakes.*

And there was a great deal more in that than you would think.

Because, five weeks later, there was a heat-wave in the Red Sea, and everybody took off all the clothes they had. The Parsee took off his hat; but the Rhinoceros took off his skin and carried it over his shoulder as he came down to the beach to bathe. In those days it buttoned underneath with three buttons and looked like a waterproof. He said nothing whatever about the Parsee's cake, because he had eaten it all; and he never had any manners, then, since, or henceforward. He waddled straight into the water and blew bubbles through his nose, leaving his skin on the beach.

Presently the Parsee came by and found the skin, and he smiled one smile that ran all round his face two times. Then he danced three times round the skin and rubbed his hands. Then he went to his camp and filled his hat with cake-crumbs, for the Parsee never

17

ate anything but cake, and never swept out his camp. He took that skin, and he shook that skin, and he scrubbed that skin, and he rubbed that skin just as full of old, dry, stale, tickly cake-crumbs and some burned currants as ever it could *possibly* hold. Then he climbed to the top of his palm-tree and waited for the Rhinoceros to come out of the water and put it on.

And the Rhinoceros did. He buttoned it up with the three buttons, and it tickled like cake-crumbs in bed. Then he wanted to scratch, but that made it worse; and then he lay down on the sands and rolled and rolled and rolled, and every time he rolled the cake crumbs tickled him worse and worse and worse. Then he ran to the palm-tree and rubbed and rubbed and rubbed himself against it. He rubbed so much and so hard that he rubbed his skin into a great fold over his shoulders, and another fold underneath, where the buttons used to be (but he rubbed the buttons off), and he rubbed some more folds over his legs. And it spoiled his temper, but it didn't make the least difference to the cake-crumbs. They were inside his skin and they tickled. So he went home, very angry indeed and horribly scratchy; and from that day to this every rhinoceros has great folds in his skin and a very bad temper, all on account of the cake-crumbs inside.

But the Parsee came down from his palm-tree, wearing his hat, from which the rays of the sun were reflected in more-than-oriental splendour, packed up his cooking-stove, and went away in the direction of Orotavo, Amygdala, the Upland Meadows of Anantarivo, and the Marshes of Sonaput.

HOW THE LEOPARD GOT HIS SPOTS

IN the days when everybody started fair, Best Beloved, the Leopard lived in a place called the High Veldt. 'Member it wasn't the Low Veldt, or the Bush Veldt, or the Sour Veldt, but the 'sclusively bare, hot, shiny High Veldt, where there was sand and sandy-coloured rock and 'sclusively tufts of sandy-yellowish grass. The Giraffe and the Zebra and the Eland and the Koodoo and the Harte-beest lived there; and they were 'sclusively sandy-yellow-brownish all over; but the Leopard, he was the 'sclusivest sandiest-yellowish-brownest of them all—a greyish-yellowish catty-shaped kind of beast, and he matched the 'sclusively yellowish-greyish-brownish colour of the High Veldt to one hair. This was very bad for the Giraffe and the Zebra and the rest of them; for he would lie down by a 'sclusively yellowish-greyish-brownish stone or clump of grass, and when the Giraffe or the Zebra or the Eland or the Koodoo or the Bush-Buck or the Bonte-Buck came by he would surprise them out of their jumpsome lives. He would indeed! And, also, there was an Ethiopian with bows and arrows (a 'sclusively greyish - brownish - yellowish man he was then), who lived on the High Veldt with the Leopard; and the two used to hunt together—the Ethiopian with his bows and arrows, and the Leopard 'sclusively with his teeth and claws—till the Giraffe and the Eland and the Koodoo and the Quagga and all the rest of them didn't know which way to jump, Best Beloved. They didn't indeed!

After a long time—things lived for ever so long in those days—they learned to avoid anything that looked like a Leopard or an Ethiopian; and bit by bit—the Giraffe began it, because his legs were the longest—they went away from the High Veldt. They scuttled for days and days and days till they came to a great forest, 'sclusively full of trees and bushes and stripy, speckly, patchy-blatchy shadows, and there they hid: and after another long time, what with standing half in the shade and half out of it, and what with the slippery-slidy shadows of the trees falling on them, the Giraffe grew blotchy, and the Zebra grew stripy, and the Eland and the Koodoo grew darker, with little wavy grey

lines on their backs like bark on a tree trunk; and so, though you could hear them and smell them, you could very seldom see them, and then only when you knew precisely where to look. They had a beautiful time in the 'sclusively speckly-spickly shadows of the forest, while the Leopard and the Ethiopian ran about over the 'sclusively greyish-yellowish-reddish High Veldt outside, wondering where all their breakfasts and their dinners and their teas had gone. At last they were so hungry that they ate rats and beetles and rock-rabbits, the Leopard and the Ethiopian, and then they had the Big Tummy-ache, both together; and then they met Baviaan — the dog-headed, barking Baboon, who is Quite the Wisest Animal in All South Africa.

20

Said Leopard to Baviaan (and it was a very hot day), 'Where has all the game gone?'

And Baviaan winked. *He* knew.

Said the Ethiopian to Baviaan, 'Can you tell me the present habitat of the aboriginal Fauna?' (That meant just the same thing, but the Ethiopian always used long words. He was a grown-up.)

And Baviaan winked. *He* knew.

Then said Baviaan, 'The game has gone into other spots; and my advice to you, Leopard, is to go into other spots as soon as you can.'

And the Ethiopian said, 'That is all very fine, but I wish to know whither the aboriginal Fauna has migrated.'

Then said Baviaan, 'The aboriginal Fauna has joined the aboriginal Flora because it was high time for a change; and my advice to you, Ethiopian, is to change as soon as you can.'

That puzzled the Leopard and the Ethiopian, but they set off to look for the aboriginal Flora, and presently, after ever so many days, they saw a great, high, tall forest full of tree trunks all 'sclusively speckled and sprottled and spottled, dotted and splashed and slashed and hatched and cross-hatched with shadows. (Say that quickly aloud, and you will see how *very* shadowy the forest must have been.)

'What is this,' said the Leopard, 'that is so 'sclusively dark, and yet so full of little pieces of light?'

'I don't know,' said the Ethiopian, 'but it ought to be the aboriginal Flora. I can smell Giraffe, and I can hear Giraffe, but I can't see Giraffe.'

'That's curious,' said the Leopard. 'I suppose it is because we have just come in out

21

of the sunshine. I can smell Zebra, and I can hear Zebra, but I can't see Zebra.'

'Wait a bit,' said the Ethiopian. 'It's a long time since we've hunted 'em. Perhaps we've forgotten what they were like.'

'Fiddle!' said the Leopard. 'I remember them perfectly on the High Veldt, especially their marrow-bones. Giraffe is about seventeen feet high, of a 'sclusively fulvous golden-yellow from head to heel; and Zebra is about four and a half feet high, of a 'sclusively grey-fawn colour from head to heel.'

'Umm,' said the Ethiopian, looking into the speckly-spickly shadows of the aboriginal Flora-forest. 'Then they ought to show up in this dark place like ripe bananas in a smoke-house.'

But they didn't. The Leopard and the Ethiopian hunted all day; and though they could smell them and hear them, they never saw one of them.

'For goodness sake,' said the Leopard at tea-time, 'let us wait till it gets dark. This daylight hunting is a perfect scandal.'

So they waited till dark, and then the Leopard heard something breathing sniffily in the starlight that fell all stripy through the branches, and he jumped at the noise, and it smelt like Zebra, and it felt like Zebra, and when he knocked it down it kicked like Zebra, but he couldn't see it. So he said, 'Be quiet, O you person without any form. I am going to sit on your head till morning, because there is something about you that I don't understand.'

Presently he heard a grunt and a crash and a scramble and the Ethiopian called out, 'I've caught a thing that I can't see. It smells like Giraffe, and it kicks like Giraffe, but it hasn't any form.'

'Don't you trust it,' said the Leopard. 'Sit on its head till the morning—same as me. They haven't any form—any of 'em.'

So they sat down on them hard till bright morning-time, and then Leopard said, 'What have you at your end of the table, Brother?'

The Ethiopian scratched his head and said, 'It ought to be 'sclusively a rich fulvous orange-tawny from head to heel, and it ought to be Giraffe; but it is covered all over with chestnut blotches. What have you at *your* end of the table, Brother?'

And the Leopard scratched his head and said, 'It ought to be 'sclusively a delicate greyish-fawn, and it ought to be Zebra; but it is covered all over with black and purple stripes. What in the world have you been doing to yourself, Zebra? Don't you know that if you were on the High Veldt I could see you ten miles off? You haven't any form.'

'Yes,' said the Zebra, 'but this isn't the High Veldt. Can't you see?'

'I can now,' said the Leopard. 'But I couldn't all yesterday. How is it done?'

'Let us up,' said the Zebra, 'and we will show you.'

They let the Zebra and the Giraffe get up; and Zebra moved away to some little thorn-bushes where the sunlight fell all stripy, and Giraffe moved off to some tallish trees where the shadows fell all blotchy.

'Now watch,' said the Zebra and the Giraffe. 'This is the way it's done. One—two—three! And where's your breakfast?'

Leopard stared, and Ethiopian stared, but all they could see were stripy shadows and blotched shadows in the forest, but never a sign of Zebra and Giraffe. They had just walked off and hidden themselves in the shadowy forest.

'Hi! Hi!' said the Ethiopian. 'That's a trick worth learning. Take a lesson by it, Leopard. You show up in this dark place like a bar of soap in a coal-scuttle.'

'Ho! Ho!' said the Leopard. 'Would it surprise you very much to know that you show up in this dark place like a mustard-plaster on a sack of coals?'

23

'To a nice working blackish-brownish colour, with a little purple in it, and touches of slaty-blue. It will be the very thing for hiding in hollows and behind trees.'

So he changed his skin then and there, and the Leopard was more excited than ever; he had never seen a man change his skin before.

'But what about me?' he said, when the Ethiopian had worked his last little finger into his fine new black skin.

'You take Baviaan's advice too. He told you to go into spots.'

'So I did,' said the Leopard. 'I went into other spots as fast as I could. I went into this spot with you, and a lot of good it has done me.'

'Oh,' said the Ethiopian, 'Baviaan didn't mean spots in South Africa. He meant spots on your skin.'

'What's the use of that?' said the Leopard.

'Think of Giraffe,' said the Ethiopian. 'Or if you prefer stripes, think of Zebra. They find their spots and stripes give them per-fect satisfaction.'

'Umm,' said the Leopard. 'I wouldn't look like Zebra—not for ever so.'

'Well, make up your mind,' said the Ethiopian, 'because I'd hate to go hunting without you, but I must if you insist on looking like a sun-flower against a tarred fence.'

'I'll take spots, then,' said the Leopard 'but

'Well, calling names won't catch dinner,' said the Ethiopian. 'The long and the little of it is that we don't match our backgrounds. I'm going to take Baviaan's advice. He told me I ought to change; and as I've nothing to change except my skin I'm going to change that.'

'What to?' said the Leopard, tremendously excited.

don't make 'em too vulgar-big. I wouldn't look like Giraffe—not for ever so.'

'I'll make 'em with the tips of my fingers,' said the Ethiopian. 'There's plenty of black left on my skin still. Stand over!'

Then the Ethiopian put his five fingers close together (there was plenty of black left on his new skin still) and pressed them all over the Leopard, and wherever the five fingers touched they left five little black marks, all close together. You can see them on any Leopard's skin you like, Best Beloved. Sometimes the fingers slipped and the marks got a little blurred; but if you look closely at any Leopard now you will see that there are always five spots—off five fat black finger-tips.

'Now you *are* a beauty!' said the Ethiopian. 'You can lie out on the bare ground and look like a heap of pebbles. You can lie out on the naked rocks and look like a piece of pudding-stone. You can lie out on a leafy branch and look like sunshine sifting through the leaves; and you can lie right across the centre of a path and look like nothing in particular. Think of that and purr!'

'But if I'm all this,' said the Leopard, 'why didn't you go spotty too?'

'Oh, plain black's best,' said the Ethiopian. 'Now come along and we'll see if we can't get even with Mr. One-Two-Three-Where's-your-Breakfast!'

So they went away and lived happily ever afterward, Best Beloved. That is all.

Oh, now and then you will hear grown-ups say, 'Can the Ethiopian change his skin or the Leopard his spots?' I don't think even grown-ups would keep on saying such a silly thing if the Leopard and the Ethiopian hadn't done it once—do you? But they will never do it again, Best Beloved. They are quite contented as they are.

THE ELEPHANT'S CHILD

IN the High and Far-Off Times the Elephant, O Best Beloved, had no trunk. He had only a blackish, bulgy nose, as big as a boot, that he could wriggle about from side to side; but he couldn't pick up things with it. But there was one Elephant—a new Elephant—an Elephant's Child—who was full of 'satiable curtiosity, and that means he asked ever so many questions. *And* he lived in Africa, and he filled all Africa with his 'satiable curtiosities. He asked his tall aunt, the Ostrich, why her tail-feathers grew just so, and his tall aunt the Ostrich spanked him with her hard, hard claw. He asked his tall uncle, the Giraffe, what made his skin spotty, and his tall uncle, the Giraffe, spanked him with his hard, hard hoof. And still he was full of 'satiable curtiosity! He asked his broad aunt, the Hippopotamus, why her eyes were red, and his broad aunt, the Hippopotamus, spanked him with her broad, broad hoof; and he asked his hairy uncle, the Baboon, why melons tasted just so, and his hairy uncle, the Baboon, spanked him with his hairy, hairy paw. And *still* he was full of 'satiable curtiosity! He asked questions about everything that he saw, or heard, or felt, or smelt, or touched, and all his uncles and his aunts spanked him. And still he was full of 'satiable curtiosity!

26

One fine morning in the middle of the Precession of the Equinoxes this 'satiable Elephant's Child asked a new fine question that he had never asked before. He asked, 'What does the Crocodile have for dinner?' Then everybody said, 'Hush!' in a loud and dretful tone, and they spanked him immediately and directly, without stopping, for a long time.

By and by, when that was finished, he came upon Kolokolo Bird sitting in the middle of a wait-a-bit thorn-bush, and he said, 'My father has spanked me, and my mother has spanked me; all my aunts and uncles have spanked me for my 'satiable curtiosity; and *still* I want to know what the Crocodile has for dinner!'

Then Kolokolo Bird said, with a mournful cry, 'Go to the banks of the great grey-green, greasy Limpopo River, all set about with fever-trees, and find out.'

That very next morning, when there was nothing left of the Equinoxes, because the Precession had preceded according to precedent, this 'satiable Elephant's Child took a hundred pounds of bananas (the little short red kind), and a hundred pounds of sugar-cane (the long purple kind), and seventeen melons (the greeny-crackly kind), and said to all his dear families, 'Good-bye. I am going to the great grey-green, greasy Limpopo River, all set about with fever-trees, to find out what the Crocodile has for dinner.' And they all spanked him once more for luck, though he asked them most politely to stop.

Then he went away, a little warm, but not at all astonished, eating melons, and throwing the rind about, because he could not pick it up.

He went from Graham's Town to Kimberley, and from Kimberley to Khama's Country, and from Khama's Country he went east by north, eating melons all the time, till at last he came to the banks of the great grey-green, greasy Limpopo River, all set about with fever-trees, precisely as Kolokolo Bird had said.

Now you must know and understand, O Best Beloved, that till that very week, and day, and hour, and minute, this 'satiable Elephant's Child had never seen a Crocodile, and did not know what one was like. It was all his 'satiable curiosity.

The first thing that he found was a Bi-Coloured-Python-Rock-Snake curled round a rock.

' 'Scuse me,' said the Elephant's Child most politely, 'but have you seen such a thing as a Crocodile in these promiscuous parts?'

'*Have* I seen a Crocodile?' said the Bi-Coloured-Python-Rock-Snake, in a voice of dretful scorn. 'What will you ask me next?'

' 'Scuse me,' said the Elephant's Child, 'but could you kindly tell me what he has for dinner?'

Then the Bi-Coloured-Python-Rock-Snake uncoiled himself very quickly from the rock, and spanked the Elephant's Child with his scalesome, flailsome tail.

'That is odd,' said the Elephant's Child, 'because my father and my mother, and my uncle and my aunt, not to mention my other aunt, the Hippopotamus, and my other uncle, the Baboon, have all spanked me for my 'satiable curtiosity—and I suppose this is the same thing.'

So he said good-bye very politely to the Bi-Coloured-Python-Rock-Snake, and helped to coil him up on the rock again, and went on, a little warm, but not at all astonished, eating melons, and throwing the rind about, because he could not pick it up, till he trod on what he thought was a log of wood at the very edge of the great grey-green, greasy Limpopo River, all set about with fever-trees.

But it was really the Crocodile, O Best Beloved, and the Crocodile winked one eye—like this!

' 'Scuse me,' said the Elephant's Child most politely, 'but do you happen to have seen a Crocodile in these promiscuous parts?'

Then the Crocodile winked the other eye, and lifted half his tail out of the mud; and the Elephant's Child stepped back most politely, because he did not wish to be spanked again.

'Come hither, Little One,' said the Crocodile. 'Why do you ask such things?'

' 'Scuse me,' said the Elephant's Child most politely, 'but my father has spanked me, my

28

mother has spanked me, not to mention my tall aunt, the Ostrich, and my tall uncle, the Giraffe, who can kick ever so hard, as well as my broad aunt, the Hippopotamus, and my hairy uncle, the Baboon, *and* including the Bi-Coloured-Python-Rock-Snake, with the scalesome, flailsome tail, just up the bank, who spanks harder than any of them; and so, if it's quite all the same to you, I don't want to be spanked any more.'

'Come hither, Little One,' said the Crocodile, 'for I am the Crocodile,' and he wept crocodile-tears to show it was quite true.

Then the Elephant's Child grew all breathless, and panted, and kneeled down on the bank and said, 'You are the very person I have been looking for all these long days. Will you please tell me what you have for dinner?'

'Come hither, Little One,' said the Crocodile, 'and I'll whisper.'

Then the Elephant's Child put his head down close to the Crocodile's musky, tusky mouth, and the Crocodile caught him by his little nose, which up to that very week, day, hour, and minute, had been no bigger than a boot, though much more useful.

'I think,' said the Crocodile—and he said it between his teeth, like this—'I think to-day I will begin with Elephant's Child!'

At this, O Best Beloved, the Elephant's Child was much annoyed, and he said, speaking through his nose, like this, 'Led go! You are hurtig be!'

Then the Bi-Coloured-Python-Rock-Snake scuffled down from the bank and said, 'My young friend, if you do not now, immediately and instantly, pull as hard as ever you can, it is my opinion that your acquaintance in the large-pattern leather ulster' (and by this he meant the Crocodile) 'will jerk you into yonder limpid stream before you can say Jack Robinson.'

This is the way Bi-Coloured-Python-Rock-Snakes always talk.

Then the Elephant's Child sat back on his little haunches, and pulled, and pulled, and pulled, and his nose began to stretch. And the Crocodile floundered into the water, making it all creamy with great sweeps of his tail, and *he* pulled, and pulled, and pulled.

And the Elephant's Child's nose kept on stretching; and the Elephant's Child spread all his little four legs and pulled, and pulled, and pulled, and his nose kept on stretching; and the Crocodile threshed his tail like an oar, and *he* pulled, and pulled, and pulled, and at each pull the Elephant's Child's nose grew longer and longer—and it hurt him hijjus!

Then the Elephant's Child felt his legs slipping, and he said through his nose, which was

now nearly five feet long, 'This is too butch for be!'

Then the Bi-Coloured-Python-Rock-Snake came down from the bank, and knotted himself in a double-clove-hitch round the Elephant's Child's hind legs, and said, 'Rash and inexperienced traveller, we will now seriously devote ourselves to a little high tension, because if we do not, it is my impression that yonder self-propelling man-of-war with the armour-plated upper deck' (and by this, O Best Beloved, he meant the Crocodile), 'will permanently vitiate your future career.'

That is the way all Bi-Coloured-Python-Rock-Snakes always talk.

So he pulled, and the Elephant's Child pulled, and the Crocodile pulled; but the Elephant's Child and the Bi-Coloured-Python-Rock-Snake pulled hardest; and at last the Crocodile let go of the Elephant's Child's nose with a plop that you could hear all up and down the Limpopo.

Then the Elephant's Child sat down most hard and sudden; but first he was careful to say 'Thank you' to the Bi-Coloured-Python-Rock-Snake; and next he was kind to his poor pulled nose, and wrapped it all up in cool banana leaves, and hung it in the great grey-green, greasy Limpopo to cool.

'What are you doing that for?' said the Bi-Coloured-Python-Rock-Snake.

' 'Scuse me,' said the Elephant's Child, 'but my nose is badly out of shape, and I am waiting for it to shrink.'

'Then you will have to wait a long time,' said the Bi-Coloured-Python-Rock-Snake. 'Some people do not know what is good for them.'

The Elephant's Child sat there for three

days waiting for his nose to shrink. But it never grew any shorter, and, besides, it made him squint. For, O Best Beloved, you will see and understand that the Crocodile had pulled it out into a really truly trunk same as all Elephants have to-day.

At the end of the third day a fly came and stung him on the shoulder, and before he knew what he was doing he lifted up his trunk and hit that fly dead with the end of it.

''Vantage number one!' said the Bi-Coloured-Python-Rock-Snake. 'You couldn't have done that with a mere-smear nose. Try and eat a little now.'

Before he thought what he was doing the Elephant's Child put out his trunk and plucked a large bundle of grass, dusted it clean against his fore-legs, and stuffed into his own mouth.

''Vantage number two!' said the Bi-Coloured-Python-Rock-Snake. 'You couldn't have done that with a mere-smear nose. Don't you think the sun is very hot here?'

'It is,' said the Elephant's Child, and before he thought what he was doing he schlooped up a schloop of mud from the banks of the great grey-green, greasy Limpopo, and slapped it on his head, where it made a cool schloopy-sloshy mud-cap all trickly behind his ears.

''Vantage number three!' said the Bi-Coloured-Python-Rock-Snake. 'You couldn't have done that with a mere-smear nose. Now how do you feel about being spanked again?'

''Scuse me,' said the Elephant's Child, 'but I should not like it at all.'

'How would you like to spank somebody?' said the Bi-Coloured-Python-Rock-Snake.

'I should like it very much indeed,' said the Elephant's Child.

'Well,' said the Bi-Coloured-Python-Rock-Snake, 'you will find that new nose of yours very useful to spank people with.'

'Thank you,' said the Elephant's Child, 'I'll remember that; and now I think I'll go home to all my dear families and try.'

So the Elephant's Child went home across Africa frisking and whisking his trunk. When he wanted fruit to eat he pulled fruit down from a tree, instead of waiting for it to fall as he used to do. When he wanted grass he plucked grass up from the ground, instead of going on his knees as he used to do. When the flies bit him he broke off the branch of a tree and used it as a fly-whisk; and he made himself a new, cool, slushy-squshy mud-cap whenever the sun was hot. When he felt lonely walking through Africa he sang to himself down his trunk, and the noise was louder than several brass bands. He went especially out of his way to find a broad Hippopotamus (she was no relation of his), and he spanked her very hard, to make sure that the Bi-Coloured-Python-Rock-Snake had spoken the truth about his new trunk. The rest of the time he picked up the melon rinds that he had dropped on his way to the Limpopo—for he was a Tidy Pachyderm.

One dark evening he came back to all his dear families, and he coiled up his trunk and said, 'How do you do?' They were very glad to see him, and immediately said, 'Come here and be spanked for your 'satiable curtiosity.'

'Pooh,' said the Elephant's Child. 'I don't think you peoples know anything about spanking; but *I* do, and I'll show you.'

Then he uncurled his trunk and knocked two of his dear brothers head over heels.

'O Bananas!' said they, 'Where did you learn that trick, and what have you done to your nose?'

'I got a new one from the Crocodile on the banks of the great grey-green, greasy Limpopo River,' said the Elephant's Child. 'I asked him what he had for dinner, and he gave me this to keep.'

'It looks very ugly,' said his hairy uncle, the Baboon.

'It does,' said the Elephant's Child. 'But it's very useful,' and he picked up his hairy uncle, the Baboon, by one hairy leg, and hove him into a hornets' nest.

Then that bad Elephant's Child spanked all his dear families for a long time, till they were very warm and greatly astonished. He pulled out his tall Ostrich aunt's tail-feathers; and he caught his tall uncle, the Giraffe, by the hind-leg, and dragged him through a thorn-bush; and he shouted at his broad aunt, the Hippopotamus, and blew bubbles into her ear when she was sleeping in the water after meals; but he never let any one touch Kolokolo bird.

At last things grew so exciting that his dear families went off one by one in a hurry to the banks of the great grey-green, greasy Limpopo River, all set about with fever-trees, to borrow new noses from the Crocodile. When they came back nobody spanked anybody any more; and ever since that day, O Best Beloved, all the Elephants you will ever see, besides all those that you won't, have trunks precisely like the trunk of the 'satiable Elephant's Child.

32

THE SING-SONG OF OLD MAN KANGAROO

NOT always was the Kangaroo as now we do behold him, but a Different Animal with four short legs. He was grey and he was woolly, and his pride was inordinate: he danced on an outcrop in the middle of Australia, and he went to the Little God Nqa.

He went to Nqa at six before breakfast, saying, 'Make me different from all other animals by five this afternoon.'

Up jumped Nqa from his seat on the sand-flat and shouted, 'Go away!'

He was grey and he was woolly, and his pride was inordinate: he danced on a rock-ledge in the middle of Australia, and he went to the Middle God Nquing.

He went to Nquing at eight after breakfast, saying, 'Make me different from all other animals; make me, also, wonderfully popular by five this afternoon.'

Up jumped Nquing from his burrow in the spinifex and shouted, 'Go away!'

He was grey and he was woolly, and his pride was inordinate: he danced on a sandbank in the middle of Australia, and he went to the Big God Nqong.

He went to Nqong at ten before dinner-time, saying, 'Make me different from all other animals; make me popular and wonderfully run after by five this afternoon.'

Up jumped Nqong from his bath in the salt-pan and shouted, 'Yes, I will!'

Nqong called Dingo—Yellow-Dog Dingo—always hungry, dusty in the sunshine, and

showed him Kangaroo. Nqong said, 'Dingo! Wake up, Dingo! Do you see that gentleman dancing on an ashpit? He wants to be popular and very truly run after. Dingo, make him so!'

Up jumped Dingo—Yellow-Dog Dingo—and said, 'What, *that* cat-rabbit?'

Off ran Dingo—Yellow-Dog Dingo—always hungry, grinning like a coal-scuttle,—ran after Kangaroo.

Off went the proud Kangaroo on his four little legs like a bunny.

This, O Beloved of mine, ends the first part of the tale!

He ran through the desert; he ran through the mountains; he ran through the salt-pans; he ran through the reed-beds; he ran through the blue gums; he ran through the spinifex; he ran till his front legs ached.

He had to!

Still ran Dingo — Yellow-Dog Dingo — always hungry, grinning like a rat-trap, never getting nearer, never getting farther, — ran after Kangaroo.

He had to!

Still ran Kangaroo — Old Man Kangaroo. He ran through the ti-trees; he ran through the mulga; he ran through the long grass; he ran through the short grass; he ran through the Tropics of Capricorn and Cancer; he ran till his hind legs ached.

He had to!

Still ran Dingo — Yellow-Dog Dingo — hungrier and hungrier, grinning like a horse-collar, never getting nearer, never getting farther; and they came to the Wollgong River.

Now, there wasn't any bridge, and there wasn't any ferry-boat, and Kangaroo didn't know how to get over; so he stood on his legs and hopped.

He had to!

He hopped through the Flinders; he hopped through the Cinders; he hopped through the deserts in the middle of Australia. He hopped like a Kangaroo.

First he hopped one yard; then he hopped three yards; then he hopped five yards; his legs growing stronger; his legs growing longer. He hadn't any time for rest or refreshment, and he wanted them very much.

Still ran Dingo—Yellow-Dog Dingo—very much bewildered, very much hungry, and wondering what in the world or out of it made Old Man Kangaroo hop.

For he hopped like a cricket; like a pea in a saucepan; or a new rubber ball on a nursery floor.

He had to!

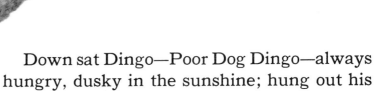

He tucked up his front legs; he hopped on his hind legs; he stuck out his tail for a balance-weight behind him; and he hopped through the Darling Downs.

He had to!

Still ran Dingo — Tired-Dog Dingo —

hungrier and hungrier, very much bewildered, and wondering when in the world or out of it would Old Man Kangaroo stop.

Then came Nqong from his bath in the salt-pans, and said, 'It's five o'clock.'

Down sat Dingo—Poor Dog Dingo—always hungry, dusky in the sunshine; hung out his tongue and howled.

Down sat Kangaroo—Old Man Kangaroo—stuck out his tail like a milking-stool behind him, and said, 'Thank goodness *that*'s finished!'

Then said Nqong, who is always a gentleman, 'Why aren't you grateful to Yellow-Dog Dingo? Why don't you thank him for all he has done for you?'

Then said Kangaroo—Tired Old Kangaroo—'He's chased me out of the homes of my childhood; he's chased me out of my regular meal-times; he's altered my shape so I'll never get it back; and he's played Old Scratch with my legs.'

Then said Nqong, 'Perhaps I'm mistaken, but didn't you ask me to make you different from all other animals, as well as to make you very truly sought after? And now it is five o'clock.'

'Yes,' said Kangaroo. 'I wish that I hadn't. I thought you would do it by charms and incantations, but this is a practical joke.'

'Joke!' said Nqong from his bath in the blue gums. 'Say that again and I'll whistle up Dingo and run your hind legs off.'

'No,' said the Kangaroo. 'I must apologise. Legs are legs, and you needn't alter 'em so far as I am concerned. I only meant to explain to Your Lordliness that I've had nothing to eat since morning, and I'm very empty indeed.'

'Yes,' said Dingo — Yellow-Dog Dingo, — 'I am just in the same situation. I've made him different from all other animals; but what may I have for my tea?'

Then said Nqong from his bath in the salt-pan, 'Come and ask me about it to-morrow, because I'm going to wash.'

So they were left in the middle of Australia, Old Man Kangaroo and Yellow-Dog Dingo, and each said, 'That's *your* fault.'

THE BEGINNING OF THE ARMADILLOS

THIS, O Best Beloved, is another story of the High and Far-Off Times. In the very middle of those times was a Stickly-Prickly Hedgehog, and he lived on the banks of the turbid Amazon, eating shelly snails and things. And he had a friend, a Slow-and-Solid Tortoise, who lived on the banks of the turbid Amazon, eating green lettuces and things. And so *that* was all right, Best Beloved. Do you see?

But also, and at the same time, in those High and Far-Off Times, there was a Painted Jaguar, and he lived on the banks of the turbid Amazon too; and he ate everything that he could catch. When he could not catch deer or monkeys he would eat frogs and beetles; and when he could not catch frogs and beetles he went to his Mother Jaguar, and she told him how to eat hedgehogs and tortoises.

She said to him ever so many times,

37

graciously waving her tail, 'My son, when you find a Hedgehog you must drop him into the water and then he will uncoil, and when you catch a Tortoise you must scoop him out of his shell with your paw.' And so that was all right, Best Beloved.

One beautiful night on the banks of the turbid Amazon, Painted Jaguar found Stickly-Prickly Hedgehog and Slow-Solid Tortoise sitting under the trunk of a fallen tree. They could not run away, and so Stickly-Prickly curled himself up into a ball, because he was a Hedgehog, and Slow-Solid Tortoise drew in his head and feet into his shell as far as they would go, because he was a Tortoise; and so *that* was all right, Best Beloved. Do you see?

'Now attend to me,' said Painted Jaguar, 'because this is very important. My mother said that when I meet a Hedgehog I am to drop him into the water and then he will uncoil, and when I meet a Tortoise I am to scoop him out of his shell with my paw. Now which of you is Hedgehog and which is Tortoise? because, to save my spots, I can't tell.'

'Are you sure of what your Mummy told you?' said Stickly-Prickly Hedgehog. 'Are you quite sure? Perhaps she said that when

you uncoil a Tortoise you must shell him out of the water with a scoop, and when you paw a Hedgehog you must drop him on the shell.'

'Are you sure of what your Mummy told you?' said Slow-and-Solid Tortoise. 'Are you quite sure? Perhaps she said that when you water a Hedgehog you must drop him into your paw, and when you meet a Tortoise you must shell him till he uncoils.'

'I don't think it was at all like that,' said Painted Jaguar, but he felt a little puzzled; 'but, please, say it again more distinctly.'

'When you scoop water with your paw you uncoil it with a Hedgehog,' said Stickly-Prickly. 'Remember that, because it's important.'

'*But*,' said the Tortoise, 'when you paw your meat you drop it into a Tortoise with a scoop. Why can't you understand?'

'You are making my spots ache,' said Painted Jaguar; 'and besides, I didn't want your advice at all. I only wanted to know which of you is Hedgehog and which is Tortoise.'

'I shan't tell you,' said Stickly-Prickly, 'but you can scoop me out of my shell if you like.'

'Aha!' said Painted Jaguar. 'Now I know you're Tortoise. You thought I wouldn't! Now I will.' Painted Jaguar darted out his paddy-paw just as Stickly-Prickly curled himself up, and of course Jaguar's paddy-paw was just filled with prickles. Worse than that, he knocked Stickly-Prickly away and away into the woods and the bushes, where it was too dark to find him. Then he put his paddy-paw into his mouth, and of course the prickles hurt him worse than ever. As soon as he could

speak he said, 'Now I know he isn't Tortoise at all. But'—and then he scratched his head with his un-prickly paw—'how do I know that this other is Tortoise?'

'But I *am* Tortoise,' said Slow-and-Solid. 'Your mother was quite right. She said that you were to scoop me out of my shell with your paw. Begin.'

'You didn't say she said that a minute ago,' said Painted Jaguar, sucking the prickles out of his paddy-paw. 'You said she said something quite different.'

'Well, suppose you say that I said that she said something quite different, I don't see that it makes any difference; because if she said what you said I said she said, it's just the same as if I said what she said she said. On the other hand, if you think she said that you were to uncoil me with a scoop, instead of pawing me into drops with a shell, I can't help that, can I?'

'But you said you wanted to be scooped out of your shell with my paw,' said Painted Jaguar.

'If you'll think again you'll find that I didn't say anything of the kind. I said that your mother said that you were to scoop me out of my shell,' said Slow-and-Solid.

'What will happen if I do?' said the Jaguar most sniffily and most cautious.

'I don't know, because I've never been scooped out of my shell before; but I tell you truly, if you want to see me swim away you've only got to drop me into the water.'

'I don't believe it,' said Painted Jaguar. 'You've mixed up all the things my mother told me to do with the things that you asked me whether I was sure that she didn't say, till I don't know whether I'm on my head or my painted tail; and now you come and tell me something I *can* understand, and it makes me more mixy than before. My mother told me that I was to drop one of you two into the water, and as you seem so anxious to be dropped I think you don't want to be dropped. So jump into the turbid Amazon and be quick about it.'

'I warn you that your Mummy won't be pleased. Don't tell her I didn't tell you,' said Slow-Solid.

'If you say another word about what my mother said—' the Jaguar answered, but he had not finished the sentence before Slow-and-Solid quietly dived into the turbid Amazon, swam under water for a long way, and came out on the bank where Stickly-Prickly was waiting for him.

'That was a very narrow escape,' said Stickly-Prickly. 'I don't like Painted Jaguar. What did you tell him that you were?'

'I told him truthfully that I was a truthful Tortoise, but he wouldn't believe it, and he made me jump into the river to see if I was, and I was, and he is surprised. Now he's gone to tell his Mummy. Listen to him!'

They could hear Painted Jaguar roaring up and down among the trees and the bushes by the side of the turbid Amazon, till his Mummy came.

40

'Son, son!' said his mother ever so many times, graciously waving her tail, 'what have you been doing that you shouldn't have done?'

'I tried to scoop something that said it wanted to be scooped out of its shell with my paw, and my paw is full of per-ickles,' said Painted Jaguar.

'Son, son!' said his mother ever so many times, graciously waving her tail, 'by the prickles in your paddy-paw I see that that must have been a Hedgehog. You should have dropped him into the water.'

'I did that to the other thing; and he said he was a Tortoise, and I didn't believe him, and it was quite true, and he has dived under the turbid Amazon, and he won't come up again, and I haven't anything at all to eat, and I think we had better find lodgings somewhere else. They are too clever on the turbid Amazon for poor me!'

'Son, son!' said his mother ever so many times, graciously waving her tail, 'now attend to me and remember what I say. A Hedgehog curls himself up into a ball and his prickles stick out every which way at once. By this you may know the Hedgehog.'

'I don't like this old lady one little bit,' said Stickly-Prickly, under the shadow of a large leaf. 'I wonder what else she knows?'

'A Tortoise can't curl himself up,' Mother Jaguar went on, ever so many times, graciously waving her tail. 'He only draws his head and legs into his shell. By this you may know the Tortoise.'

'I don't like this old lady at all—at all,' said Slow-and-Solid Tortoise. 'Even Painted Jaguar can't forget those directions. It's a great pity that you can't swim, Stickly-Prickly.'

'Don't talk to me,' said Stickly-Prickly.

'Just think how much better it would be if you could curl up. This *is* a mess! Listen to Painted Jaguar.'

Painted Jaguar was sitting on the banks of the turbid Amazon sucking prickles out of his paws and saying to himself—

'*Can't curl, but can swim—*
Slow-Solid, that's him!
Curls up, but can't swim—
Stickly-Prickly, that's him!'

'He'll never forget that this month of Sundays,' said Stickly-Prickly. 'Hold up my chin, Slow-and-Solid. I'm going to try to learn to swim. It may be useful.'

'Excellent!' said Slow-and-Solid; and he held up Stickly-Prickly's chin, while Stickly-Prickly kicked in the waters of the turbid Amazon.

'You'll make a fine swimmer yet,' said Slow-and-Solid. 'Now, if you can unlace my back-plates a little, I'll see what I can do towards curling up. It may be useful.'

Stickly-Prickly helped to unlace Tortoise's back-plates, so that by twisting and straining Slow-and-Solid actually managed to curl up a tiddy wee bit.

'Excellent!' said Stickly-Prickly; 'but I shouldn't do any more just now. It's making you black in the face. Kindly lead me into the water once again and I'll practise that side-stroke which you say is so easy.' And so Stickly-Prickly practised, and Slow-Solid swam alongside.

'Excellent!' said Slow-and-Solid. 'A little more practise will make you a regular whale. Now, if I may trouble you to unlace my back and front plates two holes more, I'll try that fascinating bend that you say is so easy. Won't Painted Jaguar be surprised!'

'Excellent!' said Stickly-Prickly, all wet from the turbid Amazon. 'I declare, I shouldn't know you from one of my own family. Two holes, I think, you said? A little more expression, please, and don't grunt quite so much, or Painted Jaguar may hear us. When you've finished, I want to try that long dive which you say is so easy. Won't Painted Jaguar be surprised!'

And so Stickly-Prickly dived, and Slow-and-Solid dived alongside.

'Excellent!' said Slow-and-Solid. 'A leetle more attention to holding your breath and you will be able to keep house at the bottom of the turbid Amazon. Now I'll try that exercise of wrapping my hind legs round my ears which you say is so peculiarly comfortable. Won't Painted Jaguar be surprised!'

'Excellent!' said Stickly-Prickly. 'But it's straining your back-plates a little. They are all overlapping now, instead of lying side by side.'

'Oh, that's the result of exercise,' said Slow-and-Solid. 'I've noticed that your prickles seem to be melting into one another, and that you're growing to look rather more like a pine-cone, and less like a chestnut-burr, than you used to.'

'Am I?' said Stickly-Prickly. 'That comes from my soaking in the water. Oh, won't Painted Jaguar be surprised!'

They went on with their exercises, each helping the other, till morning came; and when the sun was high they rested and dried themselves. Then they saw that they were both of them quite different from what they had been.

'Stickly - Prickly,' said Tortoise after breakfast, 'I am not what I was yesterday; but I think that I may yet amuse Painted Jaguar.'

'That was the very thing I was thinking just now,' said Stickly-Prickly. 'I think scales are a tremendous improvement on prickles— to say nothing of being able to swim. Oh, *won't* Painted Jaguar be surprised! Let's go and find him.'

By and by they found Painted Jaguar, still nursing his paddy-paw that had been hurt the night before. He was so astonished that he fell three times backward over his own painted tail without stopping.

'Good morning!' said Stickly-Prickly. 'And how is your dear gracious Mummy this morning?'

'She is quite well, thank you,' said Painted Jaguar; 'but you must forgive me if I do not at this precise moment recall your name.'

'That's unkind of you,' said Stickly-Prickly, 'seeing that this time yesterday you tried to scoop me out of my shell with your paw.'

'But you hadn't any shell. It was all prickles,' said Painted Jaguar. 'I know it was. Just look at my paw!'

'You told me to drop into the turbid Amazon and be drowned,' said Slow-Solid. 'Why are you so rude and forgetful to-day?'

'Don't you remember what your mother told you?' said Stickly-Prickly,—

> *'Can't curl, but can swim—*
> *Stickly-Prickly, that's him!*
> *Curls up, but can't swim—*
> *Slow-Solid, that's him!'*

Then they both curled themselves up and rolled round and round Painted Jaguar till his eyes turned truly cart-wheels in his head.

Then he went to fetch his mother.

'Mother,' he said, 'there are two new animals in the woods to-day, and the one that you said couldn't swim, swims, and the one that you said couldn't curl up, curls; and they've gone shares in their prickles, I think, because both of them are scaly all over, instead of one being smooth and the other very prickly; and, besides that, they are rolling round and round in circles, and I don't feel comfy.'

'Son, son!' said Mother Jaguar ever so many times, graciously waving her tail, 'a Hedgehog is a Hedgehog, and can't be anything but a Hedgehog; and a Tortoise is a Tortoise, and can never be anything else.'

'But it isn't a Hedgehog, and it isn't a Tortoise. It's a little bit of both, and I don't know its proper name.'

'Nonsense!' said Mother Jaguar. 'Everything has its proper name. I should call it "Armadillo" till I found out the real one. And I should leave it alone.'

So Painted Jaguar did as he was told, especially about leaving them alone; but the curious thing is that from that day to this, O Best Beloved, no one on the banks of the turbid Amazon has ever called Stickly-Prickly and Slow-Solid anything except Armadillo. There are Hedgehogs and Tortoises in other places, of course (there are some in my garden); but the real old and clever kind, with their scales lying lippety-lappety one over the other, like pine-cone scales, that lived on the banks of the turbid Amazon in the High and Far-Off Days, are always called Armadillos, because they were so clever.

So *that's* all right, Best Beloved. Do you see?

HOW THE FIRST LETTER WAS WRITTEN

ONCE upon a most early time was a Neolithic man. He was not a Jute or an Angle, or even a Dravidian, which he might well have been, Best Beloved, but never mind why. He was a Primitive, and he lived cavily in a Cave, and he wore very few clothes, and he couldn't read and he couldn't write and he didn't want to, and except when he was hungry he was quite happy. His name was Tegumai Bopsulai, and that means, 'Man-who-does-not-put-his-foot-forward-in-a-hurry'; but we, O Best Beloved, will call him Tegumai, for short. And his wife's name was Teshumai Tewindrow, and that means, 'Lady-who-asks-a-very-many-questions'; but we, O Best Beloved, will call her Teshumai, for short. And his little girl-daughter's name was Taffimai Metallumai, and that means, 'Small-person-without-any-manners-who-ought-to-be-spanked'; but I'm going to call her Taffy. And she was Tegumai Bopsulai's Best Beloved and her own Mummy's Best Beloved, and she was not spanked half as much as was good for her; and they were all three very happy. As soon as Taffy could run about she went everywhere with her Daddy Tegumai, and sometimes they would not come home to the Cave till they were hungry, and then Teshumai Tewindrow would say, 'Where in the world have you two been to, to get so shocking dirty? Really, my Tegumai, you're no better than my Taffy.'

Now attend and listen!

One day Tegumai Bopsulai went down through the beaver-swamp to the Wagai river to spear carp-fish for dinner, and Taffy went too. Tegumai's spear was made of wood with shark's teeth at the end, and before he had caught any fish at all he accidentally broke it clean across by jabbing it down too hard on the bottom of the river. They were miles and miles from home (of course they had their lunch with them in a little bag), and Tegumai had forgotten to bring any extra spears.

'Here's a pretty kettle of fish!' said Tegumai. 'It will take me half the day to mend this.'

'There's your big black spear at home,' said Taffy. 'Let me run back to the Cave and ask Mummy to give it me.'

'It's too far for your little fat legs,' said Tegumai. 'Besides, you might fall into the beaver-swamp and be drowned. We must make the best of a bad job.' He sat down and took out a little leather mendy-bag, full of reindeer-sinews and strips of leather, and lumps of bee's-wax and resin, and began to mend the spear. Taffy sat down too, with her toes in the water and her chin in her hand, and thought very hard. Then she said—

'I say, Daddy, it's an awful nuisance that you and I don't know how to write, isn't it? If we did we could send a message for the new spear.'

'Taffy,' said Tegumai, 'how often have I told you not to use slang? "Awful" isn't a pretty word,—but it *would* be a convenience, now you mention it, if we could write home.'

Just then a Stranger-man came along the river, but he belonged to a far tribe, the Tewaras, and he did not understand one word of Tegumai's language. He stood on the bank and smiled at Taffy, because he had a little girl-daughter of his own at home. Tegumai drew a hank of deer-sinews from his mendy-bag and began to mend his spear.

'Come here,' said Taffy. 'Do you know where my Mummy lives?' And the Stranger-man said 'Um!'—being, as you know, a Tewara.

'Silly!' said Taffy, and she stamped her foot, because she saw a shoal of very big carp going up the river just when her Daddy couldn't use his spear.

'Don't bother grown-ups,' said Tegumai, so busy with his spear-mending that he did not turn round.

'I aren't,' said Taffy. 'I only want him to do what I want him to do, and he won't understand.'

'Then don't bother me,' said Tegumai, and he went on pulling and straining at the deer-sinews with his mouth full of loose ends. The Stranger-man—a genuine Tewara he was—sat down on the grass, and Taffy showed him

45

what her Daddy was doing. The Stranger-man thought, 'This is a very wonderful child. She stamps her foot at me and she makes faces. She must be the daughter of that noble Chief who is so great that he won't take any notice of me.' So he smiled more politely than ever.

'Now,' said Taffy, 'I want you to go to my Mummy, because your legs are longer than mine, and you won't fall into the beaver-swamp, and ask for Daddy's other spear— the one with the black handle that hangs over our fireplace.'

The Stranger-man (and he was a Tewara) thought, 'This is a very, very wonderful child. She waves her arms and she shouts at me, but I don't understand a word of what she says. But if I don't do what she wants, I greatly fear that that haughty Chief, Man-who-turns-his-back-on-callers, will be angry.' He got up and twisted a big flat piece of bark off a birch-tree and gave it to Taffy. He did this, Best Beloved, to show that his heart was as white as the birch-bark and that he meant no harm; but Taffy didn't quite understand.

'Oh!' said she. 'Now I see! You want my Mummy's living address? Of course I can't write, but I can draw pictures if I've anything sharp to scratch with. Please lend me the shark's tooth off your necklace.'

The Stranger-man (and *he* was a Tewara) didn't say anything, so Taffy put up her little hand and pulled at the beautiful bead and seed and shark-tooth necklace round his neck.

The Stranger-man (and he *was* a Tewara) thought, 'This is a very, very, very wonderful child. The shark's tooth on my necklace is a magic shark's tooth, and I was always told that if anybody touched it without my leave they would immediately swell up or burst, but this child doesn't swell up or burst, and that important Chief, Man-who-attends-strictly-to-his-business, who has not yet taken any notice of me at all, doesn't seem to be afraid that she will swell up or burst. I had better be more polite.'

So he gave Taffy the shark's tooth, and she lay down flat on her tummy with her legs in the air, like some people on the drawing-room floor when they want to draw pictures, and she said, 'Now I'll draw you some beautiful pictures! You can look over my shoulder, but you musn't joggle. First I'll draw Daddy fishing. It isn't very like him; but Mummy will know, because I've drawn his spear all broken. Well, now I'll draw the other spear that he wants, the black-handled spear. It looks as if it was sticking in Daddy's back, but that's because the shark's tooth slipped and this piece of bark isn't big enough. That's the spear I want you to fetch; so I'll draw a picture of me myself 'splaining to you. My hair doesn't stand up like I've drawn, but it's easier to draw that way. Now I'll draw you. *I* think you're very nice really, but I can't make you pretty in the picture, so you mustn't be 'fended. Are you 'fended?'

The Stranger-man (and he was *a* Tewara) smiled. He thought, 'There must be a big battle going to be fought somewhere, and this extraordinary child, who takes my magic shark's tooth but who does not swell up or burst, is telling me to call all the great Chief's tribe to help him. He *is* a great Chief, or he would have noticed me.'

'Look,' said Taffy, drawing very hard and rather scratchily, 'now I've drawn you, and I've put the spear that Daddy wants into your hand, just to remind you that you're to bring it. Now I'll show you how to find my Mummy's living-address. You go along till you come to two trees (those are trees), and then you go over a hill (that's a hill), and then you come into a beaver-swamp all full of beavers. I haven't put in all the beavers, because I can't draw beavers, but I've drawn their heads, and that's all you'll see of them when you cross the swamp. Mind you don't fall in! Then our Cave is just beyond the beaver-swamp. It isn't as high as the hills really, but I can't draw things very small. That's my Mummy outside. She is beautiful. She is the most beautifullest Mummy there ever was, but she

won't be 'fended when she sees I've drawn her so plain. She'll be pleased of me because I can draw. Now, in case you forget, I've drawn the spear that Daddy wants *outside* our Cave. It's *inside* really, but you show the picture to my Mummy and she'll give it you. I've made her holding up her hands, because I know she'll be so pleased to see you. Isn't it a beautiful picture? And do you quite understand, or shall I 'splain again?'

The Stranger-man (and he was a *Tewara*) looked at the picture and nodded very hard. He said to himself, 'If I do not fetch this great Chief's tribe to help him, he will be slain by his enemies who are coming up on all sides with spears. Now I see why the great Chief pretended not to notice me! He feared that his enemies were hiding in the bushes and would see him deliver a message to me. Therefore he turned his back, and let the wise and wonderful child draw the terrible picture showing me his difficulties. I will away and get help for him from his tribe.' He did not even ask Taffy the road, but raced off into the bushes like the wind, with the birch-bark in his hand, and Taffy sat down most pleased.

Now this is the picture that Taffy had drawn for him!

'What have you been doing, Taffy?' said Tegumai. He had mended his spear and was carefully waving it to and fro.

'It's a little berangement of my own, Daddy dear,' said Taffy. 'If you won't ask me questions, you'll know all about it in a little time, and you'll be surprised. You don't know how surprised you'll be, Daddy! Promise you'll be surprised.'

'Very well,' said Tegumai, and went on fishing.

The Stranger-man—did you know he was a Tewara?—hurried away with the picture and ran for some miles, till quite by accident he found Teshumai Tewindrow at the door of her Cave, talking to some other Neolithic ladies who had come in to a Primitive lunch. Taffy was very like Teshumai, especially about the upper part of the face and the eyes, so the Stranger-man—always a pure Tewara—smiled politely and handed Teshumai the birch-bark. He had run hard, so that he panted, and his legs were scratched with brambles, but he still tried to be polite.

As soon as Teshumai saw the picture she screamed like anything and flew at the Stranger-man. The other Neolithic ladies at once knocked him down and sat on him in a long line of six, while Teshumai pulled his hair. 'It's as plain as the nose on this Stranger-man's face,' she said. 'He has stuck my Tegumai all full of spears, and frightened poor Taffy so that her hair stands all on end; and not content with that, he brings me a horrid picture of how it was done. Look!' She showed the picture to all the Neolithic ladies sitting patiently on the Stranger-man. 'Here is my Tegumai with his arm broken; here is a spear sticking into his back; here is a man

with a spear ready to throw; here is another man throwing a spear from a Cave, and here are a whole pack of people' (they were Taffy's beavers really, but they did look

rather like people) 'coming up behind Tegumai. Isn't it shocking!'

'Most shocking!' said the Neolithic ladies, and they filled the Stranger-man's hair with mud (at which he was surprised), and they beat upon the Reverberating Tribal Drums, and called together all the chiefs of the Tribe of Tegumai, with their Hetmans and Dolmans, all Neguses, Woons, and Akhoonds of the organisation, in addition to the Warlocks,

Angekoks, Juju-men, Bonzes, and the rest, who decided that before they chopped the Stranger-man's head off he should instantly lead them down to the river and show them where he had hidden poor Taffy.

By this time the Stranger-man (in spite of being a Tewara) was really annoyed. They had filled his hair quite solid with mud; they had rolled him up and down on knobby pebbles; they had sat upon him in a long line of six; they had thumped him and bumped him till he could hardly breathe; and though he did not understand their language, he was almost sure that the names the Neolithic ladies called him were not ladylike. However, he said nothing till all the Tribe of Tegumai were assembled, and then he led them back to the bank of the Wagai river, and there they found Taffy making daisy-chains, and Tegumai carefully spearing small carp with his mended spear.

'Well, you *have* been quick!' said Taffy. 'But why did you bring so many people? Daddy dear, this is my surprise. *Are* you surprised, Daddy?'

'Very,' said Tegumai; 'but it has ruined all my fishing for the day. Why, the whole dear, kind, nice, clean, quiet Tribe is here, Taffy.'

And so they were. First of all walked Teshumai Tewindrow and the Neolithic ladies, tightly holding on to the Stranger-man, whose hair was full of mud (although he was a Tewara). Behind them came the Head Chief, the Vice-Chief, the Deputy and Assistant Chiefs (all armed to the upper teeth), the Hetmans and Heads of Hundreds, Platoffs with their Platoons, and Dolmans with their Detachments; Woons, Neguses, and Akhoonds ranking in the rear (still armed to the teeth). Behind them was the Tribe in hierarchical order, from owners of four caves (one for each season), a private reindeer-run, and two salmon-leaps, to feudal and prognathous Villeins, semi-entitled to half a bearskin of winter nights, seven yards

from the fire, and adscript serfs, holding the reversion of a scraped marrow-bone under heriot (Aren't those beautiful words, Best Beloved?). They were all there, prancing and shouting, and they frightened every fish for twenty miles, and Tegumai thanked them in a fluid Neolithic oration.

Then Teshumai Tewindrow ran down and kissed and hugged Taffy very much indeed; but the Head Chief of the Tribe of Tegumai took Tegumai by the top-knot feathers and shook him severely.

'Explain! Explain! Explain!' cried all the Tribe of Tegumai.

'Goodness' sakes alive!' said Tegumai. 'Let go of my top-knot. Can't a man break his carp-spear without the whole countryside descending on him? You're a very interfering people.'

'I don't believe you've brought my Daddy's black-handled spear after all,' said Taffy. 'And what *are* you doing to my nice Stranger-man?'

They were thumping him by twos and threes and tens till his eyes turned round and round. He could only gasp and point at Taffy.

'Where are the bad people who speared you, my darling?' said Teshumai Tewindrow.

'There weren't any,' said Tegumai. 'My only visitor this morning was the poor fellow that you are trying to choke. Aren't you well, or are you ill, O Tribe of Tegumai?'

'He came with a horrible picture,' said the Head Chief,—'a picture that showed you were full of spears.'

'Er—um—Pr'aps I'd better 'splain that I gave him that picture,' said Taffy, but she did not feel quite comfy.

'You!' said the Tribe of Tegumai all together. 'Small-person-with-no-manners-who-ought-to-be-spanked! You?'

'Taffy dear, I'm afraid we're in for a little trouble,' said her Daddy, and put his arm round her, so she didn't care.

'Explain! Explain! Explain!' said the Head Chief of the Tribe of Tegumai, and he hopped on one foot.

'I wanted the Stranger-man to fetch Daddy's spear, so I drawded it,' said Taffy. 'There wasn't lots of spears. There was only one spear. I drawded it three times to make sure. I couldn't help it looking as if it stuck into Daddy's head—there wasn't room on the birch-bark; and those things that Mummy called bad people are my beavers. I drawded them to show him the way through the swamp; and I drawded Mummy at the mouth of the Cave looking pleased because he is a nice Stranger-man, and *I* think you are just the stupidest people in the world,' said Taffy. 'He is a very nice man. Why have you filled his hair with mud? Wash him!'

Nobody said anything at all for a long time, till the Head Chief laughed; then the Stranger-man (who was at least a Tewara) laughed; then Tegumai laughed till he fell down flat on the bank; then all the Tribe laughed more and worse and louder. The only people who did not laugh were Teshumai Tewindrow and all the Neolithic ladies. They were very polite to all their husbands, and said 'idiot!' ever so often.

Then the Head Chief of the Tribe of Tegumai cried and said and sang, 'O Small-person - without - any - manners - who - ought-to-be-spanked, you've hit upon a great invention!'

'I didn't intend to; I only wanted Daddy's black-handled spear,' said Taffy.

'Never mind. It *is* a great invention, and some day men will call it writing. At present it is only pictures, and, as we have seen to-day, pictures are not always properly understood. But a time will come, O Babe of Tegumai, when we shall make letters—all twenty-six of 'em,—and when we shall be able to read as well as to write, and then we shall always say exactly what we mean without any mistakes. Let the Neolithic ladies wash the mud out of the stranger's hair.'

'I shall be glad of that,' said Taffy, 'because, after all, though you've brought every single other spear in the Tribe of Tegumai, you've forgotten my Daddy's black-handled spear.'

Then the Head Chief cried and said and sang, 'Taffy dear, the next time you write a picture-letter, you'd better send a man who can talk our language with it, to explain what it means. I don't mind it myself, because I am a Head Chief, but it's very bad for the rest of the Tribe of Tegumai, and, as you can see, it surprises the stranger.'

Then they adopted the Stranger-man (a genuine Tewara of Tewar) into the Tribe of Tegumai, because he was a gentleman and did not make a fuss about the mud that the Neolithic ladies had put into his hair. But from that day to this (and I suppose it is all Taffy's fault), very few little girls have ever liked learning to read or write. Most of them prefer to draw pictures and play about with their Daddies—just like Taffy.

HOW THE ALPHABET WAS MADE

THE week after Taffimai Metallumai (we will still call her Taffy, Best Beloved) made that little mistake about her Daddy's spear and the Stranger-man and the picture-letter and all, she went carp-fishing again with her Daddy. Her Mummy wanted her to stay at home and help hang up hides to dry on the big drying-poles outside their Neolithic Cave, but Taffy slipped away down to her Daddy quite early, and they fished. Presently she began to giggle, and her Daddy said, 'Don't be silly, child.'

'But wasn't it inciting!' said Taffy. 'Don't you remember how the Head Chief puffed out his cheeks, and how funny the nice Stranger-man looked with the mud in his hair?'

'Well do I,' said Tegumai. 'I had to pay two deerskins—soft ones with fringes—to the Stranger-man for the things we did to him.'

'*We* didn't do anything,' said Taffy. 'It was Mummy and the other Neolithic ladies—and the mud.'

'We won't talk about that,' said her Daddy. 'Let's have lunch.'

Taffy took a marrow-bone and sat mousy-quiet for ten whole minutes, while her Daddy scratched on pieces of birch-bark with a shark's tooth. Then she said, 'Daddy, I've thinked of a secret surprise. You make a noise —any sort of noise.'

'Ah!' said Tegumai. 'Will that do to begin with?'

'Yes,' said Taffy. 'You look just like a carp-fish with its mouth open. Say it again, please.'

'Ah! ah! ah!' said her Daddy. 'Don't be rude, my daughter.'

'I'm not meaning rude, really and truly,' said Taffy. 'It's part of my secret-surprise-think. *Do* say *ah,* Daddy, and keep your mouth open at the end, and lend me that tooth. I'm going to draw a carp-fish's mouth wide-open.'

'What for?' said her Daddy.

'Don't you see?' said Taffy, scratching away on the bark. 'That will be our little secret s'prise. When I draw a carp-fish with his mouth open in the smoke at the back of our Cave—if Mummy doesn't mind—it will remind you of that ah-noise. Then we can play that it was me jumped out of the dark and s'prised you with that noise—same as I did in the beaver-swamp last winter.'

'Really?' said her Daddy, in the voice that grown-ups use when they are truly attending. 'Go on, Taffy.'

'Oh bother!' she said. 'I can't draw all of a carp-fish, but I can draw something that means a carp-fish's mouth. Don't you know how they stand on their heads rooting in the mud? Well, here's a pretence carp-fish (we can play that the rest of him is drawn). Here's just his mouth, and that means *ah.*' And she drew this. (1.)

'That's not bad,' said Tegumai, and scratched on his own piece of bark for himself; 'but you've forgotten the feeler that hangs across his mouth.'

'But I can't draw, Daddy.'

'You needn't draw anything of him except just the opening of his mouth and the feeler across. Then we'll know he's a carp-fish, 'cause the perches and trouts haven't got feelers. Look here, Taffy.' And he drew this. (2.)

'Now I'll copy it,' said Taffy. 'Will you understand *this* when you see it?' And she drew this. (3.)

'Perfectly,' said her Daddy. 'And I'll be quite as s'prised when I see it anywhere, as if you had jumped out from behind a tree and said "Ah!"'

'Now, make another noise,' said Taffy, very proud.

'Yah!' said her Daddy, very loud.

'H'm,' said Taffy. 'That's a mixy noise. The end part is *ah*-carp-fish-mouth; but what can we do about the front part? *Yer-yer-yer* and *ah! Ya!*'

'It's very like the carp-fish-mouth noise. Let's draw another bit of the carp-fish and join 'em,' said her Daddy. *He* was quite incited too.

'No. If they're joined, I'll forget. Draw it separate. Draw his tail. If he's standing on his head the tail will come first. 'Sides, I think I can draw tails easiest,' said Taffy.

'A good notion,' said Tegumai. 'Here's a carp-fish tail for the *yer*-noise.' And he drew this. (4.)

'I'll try now,' said Taffy.

53

' 'Member I can't draw like you, Daddy. Will it do if I just draw the split part of the tail, and the sticky-down line for where it joins?' And she drew this. (5.)

Her Daddy nodded, and his eyes were shiny bright with 'citement.

5

'That's beautiful,' she said. 'Now make another noise, Daddy.'

'Oh!' said her Daddy, very loud.

'That's quite easy,' said Taffy. 'You make your mouth all around like an egg or a stone. So an egg or a stone will do for that.'

'You can't always find eggs or stones. We'll have to scratch a round something like one.'

And he drew this. (6.)

'My gracious!' said Taffy, 'what a lot of noise-pictures we've made, —carp-mouth, carp-tail, and egg! Now, make another noise, Daddy.'

6

'Ssh!' said her Daddy, and frowned to himself, but Taffy was too incited to notice.

'That's quite easy,' she said, scratching on the bark.

'Eh, what?' said her Daddy. 'I meant I was thinking, and didn't want to be disturbed.'

'It's a noise just the same. It's the noise a snake makes, Daddy, when it is thinking and doesn't want to be disturbed. Let's make the ssh-noise a snake. Will this do?' And she drew this. (7.)

'There,' she said. 'That's another s'prise-secret. When you draw a

7

hissy-snake by the door of your little back-cave where you mend the spears, I'll know you're thinking hard; and I'll come in most mousy-quiet. And if you draw it on a tree by the river when you're fishing, I'll know you

want me to walk most *most* mousy-quiet, so as not to shake the banks.'

'Perfectly true,' said Tegumai. 'And there's more in this game than you think. Taffy, dear, I've a notion that your Daddy's daughter has hit upon the finest thing that there ever was since the Tribe of Tegumai took to using shark's teeth instead of flints for their spear-heads. I believe we've found out *the* big secret of the world.'

'Why?' said Taffy, and her eyes shone too with incitement.

'I'll show,' said her Daddy. 'What's water in the Tegumai language?'

'*Ya*, of course, and it means river too—like Wagai-*ya*—the Wagai river.'

'What is bad water that gives you fever if you drink it—black water—swamp-water?'

'*Yo*, of course.'

'Now look,' said her Daddy. 'S'pose you saw this scratched by the side of a pool in the beaver-swamp?' And he drew this. (8.)

'Carp-tail and round egg. Two noises mixed! *Yo*, bad water,' said Taffy. ' 'Course I wouldn't drink

8

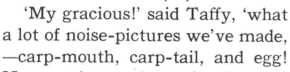

that water because I'd know you said it was bad.'

'But I needn't be near the water at all. I might be miles away, hunting, and still—'

'And *still* it would be just the same as if you stood there and said, "G'way, Taffy, or you'll get fever." All that in a carp-fish-tail and a round egg! O Daddy, we must tell Mummy, quick!' and Taffy danced all round him.

'Not yet,' said Tegumai; 'not till we've gone a little further. Let's see. *Yo* is bad water, but so is food cooked on the fire, isn't it?' And he drew this. (9.)

'Yes. Snake and egg,' said Taffy. 'So that means dinner's ready. If you saw that scratched on a tree you'd know it was time to come to the Cave. So'd I.'

'My Winkie!' said Tegumai. 'That's true too. But wait a minute. I see a difficulty. *So* means "come and have dinner," but *sho* means the drying-poles where we hang our hides.'

'Horrid old drying-poles!' said Taffy. 'I hate helping to hang heavy, hot, hairy hides on them. If you drew the snake and egg, and I thought it meant dinner, and I came in from the wood and found that it meant I was to help Mummy hang the two hides on the drying-poles, what *would* I do?'

'You'd be cross. So'd Mummy. We must make a new picture for *sho*. We must draw a spotty snake that hisses *sh-sh,* and we'll play that the plain snake only hisses ssss.'

'I couldn't be sure how to put in the spots,' said Taffy. 'And p'raps if *you* were in a hurry you might leave them out, and I'd think it was so when it was *sho,* and then Mummy would catch me just the same. *No!* I think we'd better draw a picture of the horrid high drying-poles their very selves, and make *quite* sure. I'll put them in just after the hissy-snake. Look!' And she drew this. (10.)

'P'raps that's safest. It's very like our drying-poles, anyhow,' said her Daddy, laughing. 'Now I'll make a new noise with a snake and drying-pole sound in it. I'll say *shi.* That's Tegumai for spear, Taffy.' And he laughed.

'Don't make fun of me,' said Taffy, as she thought of her picture-letter and the mud in the Stranger-man's hair. '*You* draw it, Daddy.'

'We won't have beavers or hills this time, eh?' said her Daddy. 'I'll just draw a straight line for my spear.' And he drew this. (11.)

'Even Mummy couldn't mistake that for me being killed.'

'*Please* don't, Daddy. It makes me un-comfy. Do some more noises. We're getting on beautifully.'

'Er-hm!' said Tegumai, looking up. 'We'll say *shu*. That means sky.'

Taffy drew the snake and the drying-pole. Then she stopped. 'We must make a new picture for that end sound, mustn't we?'

'*Shu-shu-u-u-u!*' said her Daddy. 'Why it's just like the round-egg-sound made thin.'

'Then s'pose we draw a thin round egg, and pretend it's a frog that hasn't eaten anything for years.'

'N-no,' said her Daddy. 'If we drew that in a hurry we might mistake it for the round egg itself. *Shu-shu-shu! I'll* tell you what we'll do. We'll open a little hole at the end of the round egg to show how the O-noise runs out all thin, *ooo-oo-oo*. Like this.' And he drew this. (12.)

12

'Oh, that's lovely! Much better than a thin frog. Go on,' said Taffy, using her shark's tooth.

Her Daddy went on drawing, and his hand shook with excite-ment. He went on till he had drawn this. (13.)

13

'Don't look up, Taffy,' he said. 'Try if you can make out what that means in the Tegumai language. If you can, we've found the Secret.'

'Snake—pole—broken-egg—carp-tail and carp-mouth,' said Taffy. '*Shu-ya*. Sky-water (rain).' Just then a drop fell on her hand, for the day had clouded over. 'Why, Daddy, it's raining. Was *that* what you meant to tell me?'

'Of course,' said her Daddy. 'And I told it you without saying a word, didn't I?'

'Well, I *think* I would have known it in a minute, but that raindrop made me quite sure. I'll always remember now. *Shu-ya* means rain or "it is going to rain." Why, Daddy!' She got up and danced round him. 'S'pose you went out before I was awake, and drawed *shu-ya* in the smoke on the wall, I'd know it was going to rain and I'd take my beaver-skin hood. Wouldn't Mummy be surprised!'

Tegumai got up and danced. (Daddies didn't mind doing those things in those days.) 'More than that! More than that!' he said. 'S'pose I wanted to tell you it wasn't going to rain much and you must come down to the river, what would we draw? Say the words in Tegumai-talk first.'

'*Shu-ya-las, ya maru.* (Sky-water ending. River come to.) *What* a lot of new sounds! *I* don't see how we can draw them.'

'But I do—but I do!' said Tegumai. 'Just attend a minute, Taffy, and we won't do any more to-day. We've got *shu-ya* all right, haven't we? but this *las* is a teaser. *La-la-la!*' and he waved his shark-tooth.

'There's the hissy-snake at the end and the carp-mouth before the snake—*as-as-as*. We only want *la-la*,' said Taffy.

'I know it, but we have to make *la la*. And we're the first people in all the world who've ever tried to do it, Taffimai!'

'Well,' said Taffy, yawning, for she was rather tired. '*Las* means breaking or finishing as well as ending, doesn't it?'

'So it does,' said Tegumai. '*Ya-las* means that there's no water in the tank for Mummy to cook with—just when I'm going hunting, too.'

'And *shi-las* means that your spear is

broken. If I'd only thought of *that* instead of drawing silly beaver pictures for the Stranger!'

'*La! La! La!*' said Tegumai, waving his stick and frowning. 'Oh bother!'

'I could have drawn *shi* quite easily,' Taffy went on. 'Then I'd have drawn your spear all broken —this way!' And she drew. (14.)

14

'The very thing,' said Tegumai. 'That's *la* all over. It isn't like any of the other marks, either.' And he drew this. (15.)

15

'Now for *ya*. Oh, we've done that before. Now for *maru*. *Mum-mum-mum*. *Mum* shuts one's mouth up, doesn't it? We'll draw a shut mouth like this.' And he drew. (16.)

16

'Then the carp-mouth open. That makes *Ma-ma-ma!* But what about this *rrrrr*-thing, Taffy?'

'It sounds all rough and edgy, like your shark-tooth saw when you're cutting out a plank for the canoe,' said Taffy.

17

'You mean all sharp at the edges, like this?' said Tegumai. And he drew. (17.)

' 'Xactly,' said Taffy. 'But we don't want all those teeth: only put two.'

'I'll only put in one,' said Tegumai. 'If this game of ours is going to be what I think it will, the easier we make our sound-pictures the better for everybody.' And he drew. (18.)

18

'*Now* we've got it,' said Tegumai, standing on one leg. 'I'll draw 'em all in a string like fish.'

'Hadn't we better put a little bit of stick or something between each word, so's they won't rub up against each other and jostle, same as if they were carps?'

'Oh, I'll leave a space for that,' said her Daddy. And very incitedly he drew them all without stopping, on a big new bit of birch-bark. (19.)

19

'*Shu-ya-las ya-maru*,' said Taffy, reading it out sound by sound.

'That's enough for to-day,' said Tegumai. 'Besides, you're getting tired, Taffy. Never mind, dear. We'll finish it all to-morrow, and then we'll be remembered for years and years after the biggest trees you can see are all chopped up for firewood.'

So they went home, and all that evening Tegumai sat on one side of the fire and Taffy on the other, drawing *ya*'s and *yo*'s and *shu*'s and *shi*'s in the smoke on the wall and giggling together till her Mummy said, 'Really, Tegumai, you're worse than my Taffy.'

'Please don't mind,' said Taffy. 'It's only our secret-s'prise, Mummy dear, and we'll tell you all about it the very minute it's done; but *please* don't ask me what it is now, or else I'll have to tell.'

So her Mummy most carefully didn't; and bright and early next morning Tegumai went down to the river to think about new sound-pictures, and when Taffy got up she saw *Ya-las* (water is ending or running out) chalked on the side of the big stone water-tank, out-side the Cave.

'Um,' said Taffy. 'These picture-sounds are rather a bother! Daddy's just as good as come here himself and told me to get more water for Mummy to cook with.' She went to the spring at the back of the house and filled the tank from a bark bucket, and then she ran down to the river and pulled her Daddy's left ear—the one that belonged to her to pull when she was good.

'Now come along and we'll draw all the left-over sound-pictures,' said her Daddy, and they had a most inciting day of it, and a beautiful lunch in the middle, and two games of romps. When they came to T, Taffy said that as her name, and her Daddy's, and her Mummy's all began with that sound, they should draw a sort of family group of them-selves holding hands. That was all very well to draw once or twice; but when it came to drawing it six or seven times, Taffy and Tegumai drew it scratchier and scratchier, till at last the T-sound was only a thin long Tegumai with his arms out to hold Taffy and Teshumai. You can see from these three pictures partly how it happened. (20, 21, 22.)

20   21   22

Many of the other pictures were much too beautiful to begin with, especially before lunch, but as they were drawn over and over again on birch-bark, they became plainer and easier, till at last even Tegumai said he could

find no fault with them. They turned the hissy-snake the other way round for the Z-sound, to show it was hissing backwards in a soft and gentle way (23); and 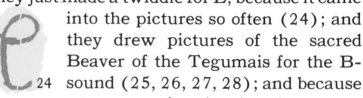 they just made a twiddle for E, because it came into the pictures so often (24); and they drew pictures of the sacred Beaver of the Tegumais for the B-sound (25, 26, 27, 28); and because it was a nasty, nosy noise, they just drew noses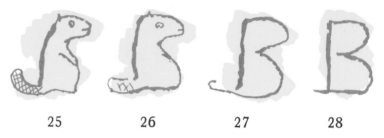

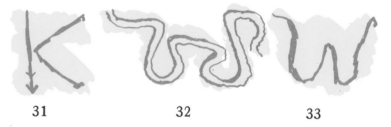

25   26   27   28

for the N-sound, till they were tired (29); and they drew a pic-ture of the big lake-pike's mouth for the greedy Ga-sound (30); and they drew the pike's mouth again with a spear behind it for the scratchy, hurty Ka-sound (31); and they drew pictures of 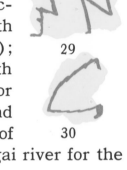 a little bit of the winding Wagai river for the

31   32   33

nice windy-windy Wa-sound (32, 33); and so on and so forth and so following till they had done and drawn all the sound-pictures that they wanted, and there was the Alphabet, all complete.

And after thousands and thousands and thousands of years, and after Hieroglyphics and Demotics, and Nilotics, and Cryptics, and Cufics, and Runics, and Dorics, and Ionics, and all sorts of other ricks and tricks (because the Woons, and the Neguses, and the Akhoonds, and the Repositories of Tradition would never leave a good thing alone when they saw it), the fine old easy, understandable Alphabet—A, B, C, D, E, and the rest of 'em—got back into its proper shape again for all Best Beloveds to learn when they are old enough.

But *I* remember Tegumai Bopsulai, and Taffimai Metallumai and Teshumai Tewindrow, her dear Mummy, and all the days gone by. And it was so—just so—a little time ago—on the banks of the big Wagai!

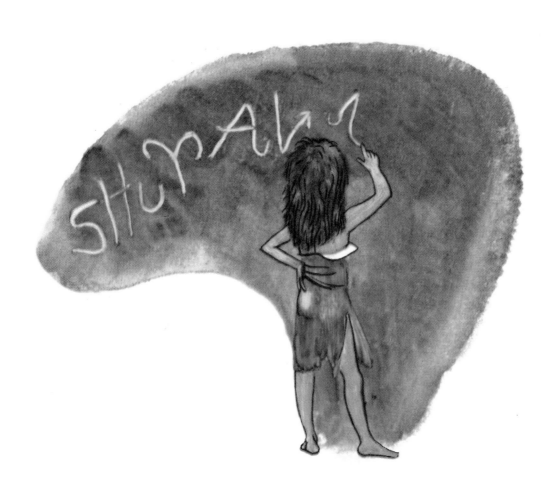

THE CRAB THAT PLAYED WITH THE SEA

BEFORE the High and Far-Off Times, O my Best Beloved, came the Time of the Very Beginnings; and that was in the days when the Eldest Magician was getting Things ready. First he got the Earth ready; then he got the Sea ready; and then he told all the Animals that they could come out and play. And the Animals said, 'O Eldest Magician, what shall we play at?' and he said, 'I will show you.' He took the Elephant—All-the-Elephant-there-was—and said, 'Play at being an Elephant,' and All-the-Elephant-there-was played. He took the Beaver—All-the-Beaver-there-was—and said, 'Play at being a Beaver,' and All-the-Beaver-there-was played. He took the Cow—All-the-Cow-there-was—and said, 'Play at being a Cow,' and All-the-Cow-there-was played. He took the Turtle—All-the-Turtle-there-was—and said, 'Play at being a Turtle,' and All-the-Turtle-there-was played. One by one he took all the beasts and birds and fishes and told them what to play at.

But towards evening, when people and things grow restless and tired, there came up the Man (With his own little girl-daughter?) —Yes, with his own best beloved little girl-daughter sitting upon his shoulder, and he said, 'What is this play, Eldest Magician?' And the Eldest Magician said, 'Ho, Son of Adam, this is the play of the Very Beginning; but you are too wise for this play.' And the

Man saluted and said, 'Yes, I am too wise for this play; but see that you make all the Animals obedient to me.'

Now, while the two were talking together, Pau Amma the Crab, who was next in the game, scuttled off sideways and stepped into the sea, saying to himself, 'I will play my play alone in the deep waters, and I will never be obedient to this son of Adam.' Nobody saw him go away except the little girl-daughter where she leaned on the Man's shoulder. And the play went on till there were no more Animals left without orders; and the Eldest Magician wiped the fine dust off his hands and walked about the world to see how the Animals were playing.

He went North, Best Beloved, and he found All-the-Elephant-there-was digging with his tusks and stamping with his feet in the nice new clean earth that had been made ready for him.

'*Kun?*' said All-the-Elephant-there-was, meaning, 'Is this right?'

'*Payah kun,*' said the Eldest Magician, meaning, 'That is quite right'; and he breathed upon the great rocks and lumps of earth that All-the-Elephant-there-was had thrown up, and they became the great Himalayan Mountains, and you can look them out on the map.

He went East, and he found All-the-Cow-there-was feeding in the field that had been made ready for her, and she licked her tongue round a whole forest at a time, and swallowed it and sat down to chew her cud.

'*Kun?*' said All-the-Cow-there-was.

'*Payah kun,*' said the Eldest Magician; and he breathed upon the bare patch where she had eaten, and upon the place where she had sat down, and one became the great Indian Desert, and the other became the Desert of Sahara, and you can look them out on a map.

He went West, and he found All-the-Beaver-there-was making a beaver-dam across the mouths of broad rivers that had been got ready for him.

'*Kun?*' said All-the-Beaver-there-was.

'*Payah kun,*' said the Eldest Magician; and

he breathed upon the fallen trees and the still water, and they became the Everglades in Florida, and you may look them out on the map.

Then he went South and found All-the-Turtle-there-was scratching with his flippers in the sand that had been got ready for him, and the sand and the rocks whirled through the air and fell far off into the sea.

'*Kun?*' said All-the-Turtle-there-was.

'*Payah kun,*' said the Eldest Magician; and he breathed upon the sand and the rocks, where they had fallen in the sea, and they became the most beautiful islands of Borneo, Celebes, Sumatra, Java, and the rest of the Malay Archipelago, and you can look *them* out on the map!

By and by the Eldest Magician met the Man on the banks of the Perak river, and said, 'Ho! Son of Adam, are all the Animals obedient to you?'

'Yes,' said the Man.

'Is all the Earth obedient to you?'

'Yes,' said the Man.

'Is all the Sea obedient to you?'

'No,' said the Man. 'Once a day and once a night the Sea runs up the Perak river and drives the sweet-water back into the forest, so that my house is made wet; once a day and once a night it runs down the river and draws all the water after it, so that there is nothing left but mud, and my canoe is upset. Is that the play you told it to play?'

'No,' said the Eldest Magician. 'That is a new and a bad play.'

'Look!' said the Man, and as he spoke the great Sea came up the mouth of the Perak river, driving the river backwards till it overflowed all the dark forests for miles and miles, and flooded the Man's house.

'This is wrong. Launch your canoe and we will find out who is playing with the Sea,' said the Eldest Magician. They stepped into the canoe; the little girl-daughter came with them; and the Man took his *kris*—a curving, wavy dagger with a blade like a flame,—and they pushed out on the Perak river. Then the Sea began to run back and back, and the canoe was sucked out of the mouth of the Perak river, past Selangor, past Malacca, past Singapore, out and out to the Island of Bingtang, as though it had been pulled by a string.

Then the Eldest Magician stood up and shouted, 'Ho! beasts, birds, and fishes, that I took between my hands at the Very Beginning and taught the play that you should play, which one of you is playing with the Sea?'

Then all the beasts, birds, and fishes said together, 'Eldest Magician, we play the plays that you taught us to play—we and our children's children. But not one of us plays with the Sea.'

Then the Moon rose big and full over the water, and the Eldest Magician said to the hunchbacked old man who sits in the Moon spinning a fishing-line with which he hopes one day to catch the world, 'Ho! Fisher of the Moon, are you playing with the Sea?'

'No,' said the Fisherman, 'I am spinning a line with which I shall some day catch the world; but I do not play with the Sea.' And he went on spinning his line.

Now there is also a Rat up in the Moon who always bites the old Fisherman's line as fast as it is made, and the Eldest Magician said to him, 'Ho! Rat of the Moon, are *you* playing with the Sea?'

And the Rat said, 'I am too busy biting through the line that this old Fisherman is

spinning. I do not play with the Sea.' And he went on biting the line.

Then the little girl-daughter put up her little soft brown arms with the beautiful white shell bracelets and said, 'O Eldest Magician! when my father here talked to you at the Very Beginning, and I leaned upon his shoulder while the beasts were being taught their plays, one beast went away naughtily into the Sea before you had taught him his play.'

And the Eldest Magician said, 'How wise are little children who see and are silent! What was the beast like?'

And the little girl-daughter said, 'He was round and he was flat; and his eyes grew upon stalks; and he walked sideways like this; and he was covered with strong armour upon his back.'

And the Eldest Magician said, 'How wise

are little children who speak truth! Now I know where Pau Amma went. Give me the paddle!'

So he took the paddle; but there was no need to paddle, for the water flowed steadily past all the islands till they came to the place called Pusat Tasek—the Heart of the Sea—where the great hollow is that leads down to the heart of the world, and in that hollow grows the Wonderful Tree, Pauh Janggi, that bears the magic twin nuts. Then the Eldest Magician slid his arm up to the shoulder through the deep warm water, and under the roots of the Wonderful Tree he touched the broad back of Pau Amma the Crab. And Pau Amma settled down at the touch, and all the Sea rose up as water rises in a basin when you put your hand into it.

'Ah!' said the Eldest Magician. 'Now I know who has been playing with the Sea;' and he called out, 'What are you doing, Pau Amma?'

And Pau Amma, deep down below, answered, 'Once a day and once a night I go out to look for my food. Once a day and once a night I return. Leave me alone.'

Then the Eldest Magician said, 'Listen, Pau Amma. When you go out from your cave the waters of the Sea pour down into Pusat Tasek, and all the beaches of all the islands are left bare, and the little fish die, and Raja Moyang Kaban, the King of the Elephants, his legs are made muddy. When you come back and sit in Pusat Tasek, the waters of the Sea rise, and half the little islands are drowned, and the Man's house is flooded, and Raja Abdullah, the King of the Crocodiles, his mouth is filled with the salt water.'

Then Pau Amma, deep down below,

laughed and said, 'I did not know I was so important. Henceforward I will go out seven times a day, and the waters shall never be still.'

And the Eldest Magician said, 'I cannot make you play the play you were meant to play, Pau Amma, because you escaped me at the Very Beginning; but if you are not afraid, come up and we will talk about it.'

'I am not afraid,' said Pau Amma, and he rose to the top of the sea in the moonlight. There was nobody in the world so big as Pau Amma—for he was the King Crab of all Crabs. Not a common Crab, but a King Crab. One side of his great shell touched the beach at Sarawak; the other touched the beach at Pahang; and he was taller than the smoke of three volcanoes! As he rose up through the branches of the Wonderful Tree he tore off one of the great twin-fruits—the magic double-kernelled nuts that make people young,—and the little girl-daughter saw it bobbing alongside the canoe, and pulled it in and began to pick out the soft eyes of it with her little golden scissors.

'Now,' said the Magician, 'make a Magic, Pau Amma, to show that you are really important.'

Pau Amma rolled his eyes and waved his legs, but he could only stir up the Sea, because, though he was a King Crab, he was nothing more than a Crab, and the Eldest Magician laughed.

'You are not so important after all, Pau Amma,' he said. 'Now, let *me* try,' and he made a Magic with his left hand—with just the little finger of his left hand—and—lo and behold, Best Beloved, Pau Amma's hard, blue-green-black shell fell off him as a husk

falls off a cocoa-nut, and Pau Amma was left all soft—soft as the little crabs that you sometimes find on the beach, Best Beloved.

'Indeed, you are very important,' said the Eldest Magician. 'Shall I ask the Man here to cut you with *kris*? Shall I send for Raja Moyang Kaban, the King of the Elephants, to pierce you with his tusks, or shall I call Raja Abdullah, the King of the Crocodiles, to bite you?'

And Pau Amma said, 'I am ashamed! Give me back my hard shell and let me go back to Pusat Tasek, and I will only stir out once a day and once a night to get my food.'

And the Eldest Magician said, 'No, Pau Amma, I will *not* give you back your shell, for you will grow bigger and prouder and stronger, and perhaps you will forget your promise, and you will play with the Sea once more.'

Then Pau Amma said, 'What shall I do? I am so big that I can only hide in Pusat Tasek, and if I go anywhere else, all soft as I am now, the sharks and the dogfish will eat me. And if I go to Pusat Tasek, all soft as I am now, though I may be safe, I can never stir out to get my food, and so I shall die.' Then he waved his legs and lamented.

'Listen, Pau Amma,' said the Eldest Magician. 'I cannot make you play the play you were meant to play, because you escaped me at the Very Beginning; but if you choose, I can make every stone and every hole and every bunch of weed in all the seas a safe Pusat Tasek for you and your children for always.'

Then Pau Amma said, 'That is good, but I do not choose yet. Look! there is that Man who talked to you at the Very Beginning. If he had not taken up your attention I should not have grown tired of waiting and run away, and all this would never have happened. What will *he* do for me?'

And the Man said, 'If you choose, I will make a Magic, so that both the deep water and the dry ground will be a home for you and your children—so that you shall be able to hide both on the land and in the sea.'

And Pau Amma said, 'I do not choose yet. Look! there is that girl who saw me running away at the Very Beginning. If she had spoken then, the Eldest Magician would have called me back, and all this would never have happened. What will *she* do for me?'

And the little girl-daughter said, 'This is a good nut that I am eating. If you choose, I will make a Magic and I will give you this pair of scissors, very sharp and strong, so that you and your children can eat cocoa-nuts like this all day long when you come up from the Sea to the land; or you can dig a Pusat Tasek for yourself with the scissors that belong to you when there is no stone or hole near by; and when the earth is too hard, by the help of these same scissors you can run up a tree.'

And Pau Amma said, 'I do not choose yet, for, all soft as I am, these gifts would not help me. Give me back my shell, O Eldest Magician, and then I will play your play.'

And the Eldest Magician said, 'I will give it back, Pau Amma, for eleven months of the year; but on the twelfth month of every year it shall grow soft again, to remind you and all your children that I can make magics, and to keep you humble, Pau Amma; for I see that if you can run both under the water and on land, you will grow too bold; and if you can climb trees and crack nuts and dig holes with your scissors, you will grow too greedy, Pau Amma.'

Then Pau Amma thought a little and said, 'I have made my choice. I will take all the gifts.'

Then the Eldest Magician made a Magic with the right hand, with all five fingers of his right hand, and lo and behold, Best Beloved, Pau Amma grew smaller and smaller and

smaller, till at last there was only a little green crab swimming in the water alongside the canoe, crying in a very small voice, 'Give me the scissors!'

And the girl-daughter picked him up on the palm of her little brown hand, and sat him in the bottom of the canoe and gave him her scissors, and he waved them in his little arms, and opened them and shut them and snapped them, and said, 'I can eat nuts. I can crack shells. I can dig holes. I can climb trees. I can breathe in the dry air, and I can find a safe Pusat Tasek under every stone. I did not know I was so important. *Kun?*' (Is this right?)

'*Payah-kun,*' said the Eldest Magician, and he laughed and gave him his blessing; and little Pau Amma scuttled over the side of the canoe into the water; and he was so tiny that he could have hidden under the shadow of a dry leaf on land or of a dead shell at the bottom of the sea.

'Was that well done?' said the Eldest Magician.

'Yes,' said the Man. 'But now we must go back to Perak, and that is a weary way to paddle. If we had waited till Pau Amma had gone out of Pusat Tasek and come home, the water would have carried us there by itself.'

'You are lazy,' said the Eldest Magician. 'So your children shall be lazy. They shall be the laziest people in the world. They shall be called the Malazy—the lazy people;' and he held up his finger to the Moon and said, 'O Fisherman, here is the Man too lazy to row home. Pull his canoe home with your line, Fisherman.'

'No,' said the Man. 'If I am to be lazy all my days, let the Sea work for me twice a day for ever. That will save paddling.'

And the Eldest Magician laughed and said, '*Payah kun*' (That is right).

And the Rat of the Moon stopped biting the line; and the Fisherman let his line down till it touched the Sea, and he pulled the whole deep Sea along, past the Island of Bintang, past Singapore, past Malacca, past Selangor, till the canoe whirled into the mouth of the Perak river again.

'*Kun?*' said the Fisherman of the Moon.

'*Payah kun,*'said the Eldest Magician. 'See now that you pull the Sea twice a day and twice a night for ever, so that the Malazy fishermen may be saved paddling. But be careful not to do it too hard, or I shall make a magic on you as I did to Pau Amma.'

Then they all went up the Perak river and went to bed, Best Beloved.

Now listen and attend!

From that day to this the Moon has always pulled the sea up and down and made what we call the tides. Sometimes the Fisher of the Sea pulls a little too hard, and then we get springtides; and sometimes he pulls a little too softly, and then we get what are called neaptides; but nearly always he is careful, because of the Eldest Magician.

And Pau Amma? You can see when you go to the beach, how all Pau Amma's babies make little Pusat Taseks for themselves under every stone and bunch of weed on the sands; you can see them waving their little scissors; and in some parts of the world they truly live on the dry land and run up the palm trees and eat cocoa-nuts, exactly as the girl-daughter promised. But once a year all Pau Ammas must shake off their hard armour and be soft—to remind them of what the Eldest Magician could do. And so it isn't fair to kill or hunt Pau Amma's babies just because old Pau Amma was stupidly rude a very long time ago.

Oh yes! And Pau Amma's babies hate being taken out of their little Pusat Taseks and brought home in pickle-bottles. That is why they nip you with their scissors, and it serves you right!

THE CAT THAT WALKED BY HIMSELF

HEAR and attend and listen; for this befell and behappened and became and was, O my Best Beloved, when the Tame animals were wild. The Dog was wild, and the Horse was wild, and the Cow was wild, and the Sheep was wild, and the Pig was wild—as wild as wild could be—and they walked in the Wet Wild Woods by their wild lones. But the wildest of all the wild animals was the Cat. He walked by himself, and all places were alike to him.

Of course the Man was wild too. He was dreadfully wild. He didn't even begin to be tame till he met the Woman, and she told him that she did not like living in his wild ways. She picked out a nice dry Cave, instead of a heap of wet leaves, to lie down in; and she strewed clean sand on the floor; and she lit a nice fire of wood at the back of the Cave; and she hung a dried wild-horse skin, tail-down, across the opening of the Cave; and she said,

'Wipe your feet, dear, when you come in, and now we'll keep house.'

That night, Best Beloved, they ate wild sheep roasted on the hot stones, and flavoured with wild garlic and wild pepper; and wild duck stuffed with wild rice and wild fenugreek and wild coriander; and marrow-bones of wild oxen; and wild cherries, and wild grenadillas. Then the Man went to sleep in front of the fire ever so happy; but the Woman sat up, combing her hair. She took the bone of the shoulder of mutton—the big fat blade-bone—and she looked at the wonderful marks on it, and she threw more wood on the fire, and she made a Magic. She made the First Singing Magic in the world.

Out in the Wet Wild Woods all the wild animals gathered together where they could see the light of the fire a long way off, and they wondered what it meant.

Then Wild Horse stamped with his wild

69

foot and said, 'O my Friends and O my Enemies, why have the Man and the Woman made that great light in that great Cave, and what harm will it do us?'

Wild Dog lifted up his wild nose and smelled the smell of roast mutton, and said, 'I will go up and see and look, and say; for I think it is good. Cat, come with me.'

'Nenni!' said the Cat. 'I am the Cat who walks by himself, and all places are alike to me. I will not come.'

'Then we can never be friends again,' said Wild Dog, and he trotted off to the Cave. But when he had gone a little way the Cat said to himself, 'All places are alike to me. Why should I not go too and see and look and come away at my own liking.' So he slipped after Wild Dog softly, very softly, and hid himself where he could hear everything.

When Wild Dog reached the mouth of the Cave he lifted up the dried horse-skin with his nose and sniffed the beautiful smell of the roast mutton, and the Woman, looking at the blade-bone, heard him, and laughed, and said, 'Here comes the first. Wild Thing out of the Wild Woods, what do you want?'

Wild Dog said, 'O my Enemy and Wife of my Enemy, what is this that smells so good in the Wild Woods?'

Then the Woman picked up a roasted mutton-bone and threw it to Wild Dog, and said, 'Wild Thing out of the Wild Woods, taste and try.' Wild Dog gnawed the bone, and it was more delicious than anything he had ever tasted, and he said, 'O my Enemy and Wife of my Enemy, give me another.'

The Woman said, 'Wild Thing out of the Wild Woods, help my Man to hunt through the day and guard this Cave at night, and I will give you as many roast bones as you need.'

'Ah!' said the Cat, listening. 'This is a very wise Woman, but she is not so wise as I am.'

Wild Dog crawled into the Cave and laid his head on the Woman's lap, and said, 'O my Friend and Wife of my Friend, I will help your Man to hunt through the day, and at night I will guard your Cave.'

'Ah!' said the Cat, listening. 'That is a very foolish Dog.' And he went back through the Wet Wild Woods waving his wild tail, and walking by his wild lone. But he never told anybody.

When the Man waked up he said, 'What is Wild Dog doing here?' And the Woman said, 'His name is not Wild Dog any more, but the First Friend, because he will be our friend for always and always and always. Take him with you when you go hunting.'

Next night the Woman cut great green armfuls of fresh grass from the water-meadows, and dried it before the fire, so that it smelt like new-mown hay, and she sat at the mouth of the Cave and plaited a halter out of horse-hide, and she looked at the shoulder of mutton-bone—at the big broad blade-bone—and she made a Magic. She made the Second Singing Magic in the world.

Out in the Wild Woods all the wild animals wondered what had happened to Wild Dog, and at last Wild Horse stamped with his foot and said, 'I will go and see and say why Wild Dog has not returned. Cat, come with me.'

'Nenni!' said the Cat. 'I am the Cat who walks by himself, and all places are alike to me. I will not come.' But all the same he followed Wild Horse softly, very softly, and hid himself where he could hear everything.

When the Woman heard Wild Horse tripping and stumbling on his long mane, she laughed and said, 'Here comes the second. Wild Thing out of the Wild Woods, what do you want?'

Wild Horse said, 'O my Enemy and Wife of my Enemy, where is Wild Dog?'

The Woman laughed, and picked up the blade-bone and looked at it, and said, 'Wild Thing out of the Wild Woods, you did not come here for Wild Dog, but for the sake of this good grass.'

And Wild Horse, tripping and stumbling on his long mane, said, 'That is true; give it me to eat.'

The Woman said, 'Wild Thing out of the Wild Woods, bend your wild head and wear what I give you, and you shall eat the wonderful grass three times a day.'

'Ah,' said the Cat, listening, 'this is a clever Woman, but she is not so clever as I am.'

Wild Horse bent his wild head, and the Woman slipped the plaited hide halter over it, and Wild Horse breathed on the Woman's feet and said, 'O my Mistress, and Wife of my Master, I will be your servant for the sake of the wonderful grass.'

'Ah,' said the Cat, listening, 'that is a very foolish Horse.' And he went back through the Wet Wild Woods, waving his wild tail and walking by his wild lone. But he never told anybody.

When the Man and the Dog came back from hunting, the Man said, 'What is Wild Horse doing here?' And the Woman said, 'His name is not Wild Horse any more, but the First Servant, because he will carry us from place to place for always and always and always. Ride on his back when you go hunting.'

Next day, holding her wild head high that her wild horns should not catch in the wild trees, Wild Cow came up to the Cave, and the Cat followed, and hid himself just the same as

71

before; and everything happened just the same as before; and the Cat said the same things as before, and when Wild Cow had promised to give her milk to the Woman every day in exchange for the wonderful grass, the Cat went back through the Wet Wild Woods waving his wild tail and walking by his wild lone, just the same as before. But he never told anybody. And when the Man and the Horse and the Dog came home from hunting and asked the same questions same as before, the Woman said, 'Her name is not Wild Cow any more, but the Giver of Good Food. She will give us the warm white milk for always and always and always, and I will take care of her while you and the First Friend and the First Servant go hunting.'

Next day the Cat waited to see if any other Wild thing would go up to the Cave, but no one moved in the Wet Wild Woods, so the Cat walked there by himself; and he saw the Woman milking the Cow, and he saw the light of the fire in the Cave, and he smelt the smell of the warm white milk.

Cat said, 'O my Enemy and Wife of my Enemy, where did Wild Cow go?'

The Woman laughed and said, 'Wild Thing out of the Wild Woods, go back to the Woods again, for I have braided up my hair, and I have put away the magic blade-bone, and we have no more need of either friends or servants in our Cave.'

Cat said, 'I am not a friend, and I am not a servant. I am the Cat who walks by himself, and I wish to come into your cave.'

Woman said, 'Then why did you not come with First Friend on the first night?'

Cat grew very angry and said, 'Has Wild Dog told tales of me?'

72

Then the Woman laughed and said, 'You are the Cat who walks by himself, and all places are alike to you. You are neither a friend nor a servant. You have said it yourself. Go away and walk by yourself in all places alike.'

Then Cat pretended to be sorry and said, 'Must I never come into the Cave? Must I never sit by the warm fire? Must I never drink the warm white milk? You are very wise and very beautiful. You should not be cruel even to a Cat.'

Woman said, 'I knew I was wise, but I did not know I was beautiful. So I will make a bargain with you. If ever I say one word in your praise you may come into the Cave.'

'And if you say two words in my praise?' said the Cat.

'I never shall,' said the Woman, 'but if I say two words in your praise, you may sit by the fire in the Cave.'

'And if you say three words?' said the Cat.

'I never shall,' said the Woman, 'but if I say three words in your praise, you may drink the warm white milk three times a day for always and always and always.'

Then the Cat arched his back and said,

'Now let the Curtain at the mouth of the Cave, and the Fire at the back of the Cave, and the Milk-pots that stand beside the Fire, remember what my Enemy and the Wife of my Enemy has said.' And he went away through the Wet Wild Woods waving his wild tail and walking by his wild lone.

That night when the Man and the Horse and the Dog came home from hunting, the Woman did not tell them of the bargain that she had made with the Cat, because she was afraid that they might not like it.

Cat went far and far away and hid himself in the Wet Wild Woods by his wild lone for a long time till the Woman forgot all about him. Only the Bat—the little upside-down Bat—that hung inside the Cave, knew where Cat hid; and every evening Bat would fly to Cat with news of what was happening.

One evening Bat said, 'There is a Baby in the Cave. He is new and pink and fat and small, and the Woman is very fond of him.'

'Ah,' said the Cat, listening, 'but what is the Baby fond of?'

'He is fond of things that are soft and tickle,' said the Bat. 'He is fond of warm things to hold in his arms when he goes to sleep. He is fond of being played with. He is fond of all those things.'

'Ah,' said the Cat, listening, 'then my time has come.'

Next night Cat walked through the Wet Wild Woods and hid very near the Cave till morning-time, and Man and Dog and Horse went hunting. The Woman was busy cooking that morning, and the Baby cried and interrupted. So she carried him outside the Cave and gave him a handful of pebbles to play with. But still the Baby cried.

Then the Cat put out his paddy paw and patted the Baby on the cheek, and it cooed; and the Cat rubbed against its fat knees and tickled it under its fat chin with his tail. And the Baby laughed and the Woman heard him and smiled.

Then the Bat—the little upside-down Bat—that hung in the mouth of the Cave said, 'O my Hostess and Wife of my Host and Mother of my Host's Son, a Wild Thing from the Wild Woods is most beautifully playing with your Baby.'

'A blessing on that Wild Thing whoever he may be,' said the Woman, straightening her back, 'for I was a busy woman this morning and he has done me a service.'

The very minute and second, Best Beloved, the dried horse-skin Curtain that was stretched tail-down at the mouth of the Cave fell down—*woosh!*—because it remembered the bargain she had made with the Cat, and when the Woman went to pick it up—lo and behold!—the Cat was sitting quite comfy inside the Cave.

'O my Enemy and Wife of my Enemy and Mother of my Enemy,' said the Cat, 'it is I: for you have spoken a word in my praise, and now I can sit within the Cave for always and always and always. But still I am the Cat who walks by himself, and all places are alike to me.'

The Woman was very angry, and shut her lips tight and took up her spinning-wheel and began to spin.

But the Baby cried because the Cat had gone away, and the Woman could not hush it, for it struggled and kicked and grew black in the face.

'O my Enemy and Wife of my Enemy and Mother of my Enemy,' said the Cat, 'take a strand of the wire that you are spinning and tie it to your spinning-whorl and drag it along the floor, and I will show you a magic that shall make your Baby laugh as loudly as he is now crying.'

'I will do so,' said the Woman, 'because I am at my wits' end; but I will not thank you for it.'

She tied the thread to the little clay spindle-whorl and drew it across the floor, and the Cat ran after it and patted it with his paws and rolled head over heels, and tossed it backward over his shoulder and chased it between his hind-legs and pretended to lose it, and pounced down upon it again, till the Baby laughed as loudly as it had been crying, and scrambled

74

after the Cat and frolicked all over the Cave till it grew tired and settled down to sleep with the Cat in its arms.

'Now,' said the Cat, 'I will sing the Baby a song that shall keep him asleep for an hour.' And he began to purr, loud and low, low and loud, till the Baby fell fast asleep. The Woman smiled as she looked down upon the two of them and said, 'That was wonderfully done. No question but you are very clever, O Cat.'

That very minute and second, Best Beloved, the smoke of the fire at the back of the Cave came down in clouds from the roof—*puff!*—because it remembered the bargain she had made with the Cat, and when it had cleared away—lo and behold!—the Cat was sitting quite comfy close to the fire.

'O my Enemy and Wife of my Enemy and Mother of my Enemy,' said the Cat, 'it is I, for you have spoken a second word in my praise, and now I can sit by the warm fire at the back of the Cave for always and always and always. But still I am the Cat who walks by himself, and all places are alike to me.'

Then the Woman was very very angry, and let down her hair and put more wood on the fire and brought out the broad blade-bone of the shoulder of mutton and began to make a Magic that should prevent her from saying a third word in praise of the Cat. It was not a

Singing Magic, Best Beloved, it was a Still Magic; and by and by the Cave grew so still that a little wee-wee mouse crept out of a corner and ran across the floor.

'O my Enemy and Wife of my Enemy and Mother of my Enemy,' said the Cat, 'is that little mouse part of your magic?'

'Ouh! Chee! No indeed!' said the Woman, and she dropped the blade-bone and jumped upon the footstool in front of the fire and braided up her hair very quick for fear that the mouse should run up it.

'Ah,' said the Cat, watching, 'then the mouse will do me no harm if I eat it?'

'No,' said the Woman, braiding up her hair, 'eat it quickly and I will ever be grateful to you.'

Cat made one jump and caught the little mouse, and the Woman said, 'A hundred thanks. Even the First Friend is not quick enough to catch little mice as you have done. You must be very wise.'

That very moment and second, O Best Beloved, the Milk-pot that stood by the fire cracked in two pieces—*ffft*—because it remembered the bargain she had made with the Cat, and when the Woman jumped down from the footstool—lo and behold!—the Cat was lapping up the warm white milk that lay in one of the broken pieces.

'O my Enemy and Wife of my Enemy and Mother of my Enemy,' said the Cat, 'it is I; for you have spoken three words in my praise, and now I can drink the warm white milk three times a day for always and always and always. But *still* I am the Cat who walks by himself, and all places are alike to me.'

Then the Woman laughed and set the Cat a bowl of the warm white milk and said, 'O Cat, you are as clever as a man, but remember that your bargain was not made with the Man or the Dog, and I do not know what they will do when they come home.'

'What is that to me?' said the Cat. 'If I have my place in the Cave by the fire and my warm white milk three times a day I do not care what the Man or the Dog can do.'

That evening when the Man and the Dog came into the Cave, the Woman told them all the story of the bargain while the Cat sat by the fire and smiled. Then the Man said, 'Yes, but he has not made a bargain with *me* or with all proper Men after me.' Then he took off his two leather boots and he took up his little stone axe (that makes three) and he fetched a piece of wood and a hatchet (that is five altogether), and he set them out in a row and he said, 'Now we will make *our* bargain. If you do not catch mice when you are in the Cave for always and always and always, I will throw these five things at you whenever I see you, and so shall all proper Men do after me.'

'Ah,' said the Woman, listening, 'this is a very clever Cat, but he is not so clever as my Man.'

The Cat counted the five things (and they

looked very knobby) and he said, 'I will catch mice when I am in the Cave for always and always and always; but *still* I am the Cat who walks by himself, and all places are alike to me.'

'Not when I am near,' said the Man. 'If you had not said that last I would have put all these things away for always and always and always; but I am now going to throw my two boots and my little stone axe (that makes three) at you whenever I meet you. And so shall all proper Men do after me!'

Then the Dog said, 'Wait a minute. He has not made a bargain with *me* or with all proper Dogs after me.' And he showed his teeth and said, 'If you are not kind to the Baby while I am in the Cave for always and always and always, I will hunt you till I catch you, and when I catch you I will bite you. And so shall all proper Dogs do after me.'

'Ah,' said the Woman, listening, 'this is a very clever Cat, but he is not so clever as the Dog.'

Cat counted the Dog's teeth (and they looked very pointed) and he said, 'I will be kind to the Baby while I am in the Cave, as long as he does not pull my tail too hard, for always and always and always. But *still* I am the Cat that walks by himself, and all places are alike to me.'

'Not when I am near,' said the Dog. 'If you had not said that last I would have shut my mouth for always and always and always; but *now* I am going to hunt you up a tree whenever I meet you. And so shall all proper Dogs do after me.'

Then the Man threw his two boots and his little stone axe (that makes three) at the Cat, and the Cat ran out of the Cave and the Dog chased him up a tree; and from that day to this, Best Beloved, three proper Men out of five will always throw things at a Cat whenever they meet him, and all proper Dogs will chase him up a tree. But the Cat keeps his side of the bargain too. He will kill mice and he will be kind to Babies when he is in the house, just as long as they do not pull his tail too hard. But when he has done that, and between times, and when the moon gets up and night comes, he is the Cat that walks by himself, and all places are alike to him. Then he goes out to the Wet Wild Woods or up the Wet Wild Trees or on the Wet Wild Roofs, waving his wild tail and walking by his wild lone.

THE BUTTERFLY THAT STAMPED

THIS, O my Best Beloved, is a story—a new and a wonderful story—a story quite different from the other stories—a story about The Most Wise Sovereign Suleiman-bin-Daoud—Solomon the Son of David.

There are three hundred and fifty-five stories about Suleiman-bin-Daoud; but this is not one of them. It is not the story of the Lapwing who found the Water; or the Hoopoe who shaded Suleiman-bin-Daoud from the heat. It is not the story of the Glass Pavement, or the Ruby with the Crooked Hole, or the Gold Bars of Balkis. It is the story of the Butterfly that Stamped.

Now attend all over again and listen!

Suleiman-bin-Daoud was wise. He understood what the beasts said, what the birds said, what the fishes said, and what the insects said. He understood what the rocks said deep under the earth when they bowed in towards each other and groaned; and he understood what the trees said when they rustled in the middle of the morning. He understood everything, from the bishop on the bench to the hyssop on

the wall, and Balkis, his Head Queen, the Most Beautiful Queen Balkis, was nearly as wise as he was.

Suleiman-bin-Daoud was strong. Upon the third finger of the right hand he wore a ring. When he turned it once, Afrits and Djinns came out of the earth to do whatever he told them. When he turned it twice, Fairies came down from the sky to do whatever he told them; and when he turned it three times, the very great angel Azrael of the Sword came dressed as a water-carrier, and told him the news of the three worlds,—Above—Below—and Here.

And yet Suleiman-bin-Daoud was not proud. He very seldom showed off, and when he did he was sorry for it. Once he tried to feed all the animals in all the world in one day, but when the food was ready an Animal came out of the deep sea and ate it up in three mouthfuls. Suleiman-bin-Daoud was very surprised and said, 'O Animal, who are you?' And the Animal said, 'O King, live for ever! I am the smallest of thirty thousand brothers,

77

marry ever so many more just to show that he was the King.

Some of the wives were nice, but some were simply horrid, and the horrid ones quarrelled with the nice ones and made them horrid too, and then they would all quarrel with Suleiman-bin-Daoud, and that was horrid for him. But Balkis the Most Beautiful never quarrelled with Suleiman-bin-Daoud. She loved him too much. She sat in her rooms in the Golden Palace, or walked in the Palace garden, and was truly sorry for him.

Of course if he had chosen to turn his ring on his finger and call up the Djinns and the Afrits they would have magicked all those nine hundred and ninety-nine quarrelsome wives into white mules of the desert or greyhounds or pomegranate seeds; but Suleiman-bin-Daoud thought that that would be showing off. So, when they quarrelled too much, he only walked by himself in one part of the beautiful Palace gardens and wished he had never been born.

One day, when they had quarrelled for three weeks — all nine hundred and ninety-nine wives together — Suleiman-bin-Daoud went out for peace and quiet as usual; and among the orange trees he met Balkis the Most Beautiful, very sorrowful because Suleiman-bin-Daoud was so worried. And she said to him, 'O my Lord and Light of my Eyes, turn the ring upon your finger and show these Queens of Egypt and Mesopotamia and Persia and China that you are the great and terrible King.' But Suleiman-bin-Daoud shook his head and said, 'O my Lady and Delight of my Life, remember the Animal that came out of the sea and made me ashamed before all the animals in all the world because I showed off.

and our home is at the bottom of the sea. We heard that you were going to feed all the animals in all the world, and my brothers sent me to ask when dinner would be ready.' Suleiman-bin-Daoud was more surprised than ever and said, 'O Animal, you have eaten all the dinner that I made ready for all the animals in the world.' And the Animal said, 'O King, live for ever, but do you really call that a dinner? Where I come from we eat twice as much as that between meals.' Then Suleiman-bin-Daoud fell flat on his face and said, 'O Animal! I gave that dinner to show what a great and rich king I was, and not because I really wanted to be kind to the animals. Now I am ashamed, and it serves me right.' Suleiman-bin-Daoud was a really truly wise man, Best Beloved. After that he never forgot that it was silly to show off; and now the real story part of my story begins.

He married ever so many wives. He married nine hundred and ninety-nine wives, besides the Most Beautiful Balkis; and they all lived in a great golden palace in the middle of a lovely garden with fountains. He didn't really want nine-hundred and ninety-nine wives, but in those days everybody married ever so many wives, and of course the King had to

78

Now, if I showed off before these Queens of Persia and Egypt and Abyssinia and China, merely because they worry me, I might be made even more ashamed than I have been.'

And Balkis the Most Beautiful said, 'O my Lord and Treasure of my Soul, what will you do?'

And Suleiman-bin-Daoud said, 'O my Lady and Content of my Heart, I shall continue to endure my fate at the hands of these nine hundred and ninety-nine Queens who vex me with their continual quarrelling.'

So he went on between the lilies and the loquats and the roses and the cannas and the heavy-scented ginger-plants that grew in the garden, till he came to the great camphor-tree that was called the Camphor Tree of Suleiman-bin-Daoud. But Balkis hid among the tall irises and the spotted bamboos and the red lilies behind the camphor-tree, so as to be near her own true love, Suleiman-bin-Daoud.

Presently two Butterflies flew under the tree, quarrelling.

Suleiman-bin-Daoud heard one say to the other, 'I wonder at your presumption in talking like this to me. Don't you know that if I stamped with my foot all Suleiman-bin-Daoud's Palace and his garden here would immediately vanish in a clap of thunder.'

Then Suleiman-bin-Daoud forgot his nine hundred and ninety-nine bothersome wives, and laughed, till the camphor-tree shook, at the Butterfly's boast. And he held out his finger and said, 'Little man, come here.'

The Butterfly was dreadfully frightened, but he managed to fly up to the hand of Suleiman-bin-Daoud, and clung there, fanning himself. Suleiman-bin-Daoud bent his head and whispered very softly, 'Little man, you know that all your stamping wouldn't bend one blade of grass. What made you tell that awful fib to your wife?—for doubtless she is your wife.'

The Butterfly looked at Suleiman-bin-Daoud and saw the most wise King's eye twinkle like stars on a frosty night, and he picked up his courage with both wings, and he put his head on one side and said, 'O King, live for ever. She *is* my wife; and you know what wives are like.'

Suleiman-bin-Daoud smiled in his beard and said, 'Yes, *I* know, little brother.'

'One must keep them in order somehow,' said the Butterfly, 'and she has been quarrelling with me all the morning. I said that to quiet her.'

And Suleiman-bin-Daoud said, 'May it quiet her. Go back to your wife, little brother, and let me hear what you say.'

Back flew the Butterfly to his wife, who was all of a twitter behind a leaf, and she said, 'He heard you! Suleiman-bin-Daoud himself heard you!'

'Heard me!' said the Butterfly. 'Of course he did. I meant him to hear me.'

'And what did he say? Oh, what did he say?'

'Well,' said the Butterfly, fanning himself most importantly, 'between you and me, my dear—of course I don't blame him, because his Palace must have cost a great deal and the oranges are just ripening,—he asked me not to stamp, and I promised I wouldn't.'

'Gracious!' said his wife, and sat quite quiet; but Suleiman-bin-Daoud laughed till the tears ran down his face at the impudence of the bad little Butterfly.

Balkis the Most Beautiful stood up behind

the tree among the red lilies and smiled to herself, for she had heard all this talk. She thought, 'If I am wise I can yet save my Lord from the persecutions of these quarrelsome Queens,' and she held out her finger and whispered softly to the Butterfly's Wife, 'Little woman, come here.' Up flew the Butterfly's Wife, very frightened, and clung to Balkis's white hand.

Balkis bent her beautiful head down and whispered, 'Little woman, do you believe what your husband has just said?'

The Butterfly's Wife looked at Balkis, and saw the most beautiful Queen's eyes shining like deep pools with starlight on them, and she picked up her courage with both wings and said, 'O Queen, be lovely for ever. *You* know what men-folk are like.'

And the Queen Balkis, the Wise Balkis of Sheba, put her hand to her lips to hide a smile and said, 'Little sister, *I* know.'

'They get angry,' said the Butterfly's Wife, fanning herself quickly, 'over nothing at all, but we must humour them, O Queen. They never mean half they say. If it pleases my husband to believe that I believe he can make Suleiman-bin-Daoud's Palace disappear by stamping his foot, I'm sure *I* don't care. He'll forget all about it to-morrow.'

'Little sister,' said Balkis, 'you are quite right; but next time he begins to boast, take him at his word. Ask him to stamp, and see what will happen. *We* know what men-folk are like, don't we? He'll be very much ashamed.'

Away flew the Butterfly's Wife to her hus-

band, and in five minutes they were quarrelling worse than ever.

'Remember!' said the Butterfly. 'Remember what I can do if I stamp my foot.'

'I don't believe you one little bit,' said the Butterfly's Wife. 'I should very much like to see it done. Suppose you stamp now.'

'I promised Suleiman-bin-Daoud that I wouldn't,' said the Butterfly, 'and I don't want to break my promise.'

'It wouldn't matter if you did,' said his wife. 'You couldn't bend a blade of grass with your stamping. I dare you to do it,' she said. 'Stamp! Stamp! Stamp!'

Suleiman-bin-Daoud, sitting under the camphor-tree, heard every word of this, and he laughed as he had never laughed in his life before. He forgot all about his Queens; he forgot all about the Animal that came out of the sea; he forgot about showing off. He just laughed with joy, and Balkis, on the other side of the tree, smiled because her own true love was so joyful.

Presently the Butterfly, very hot and puffy, came whirling back under the shadow of the camphor-tree and said to Suleiman, 'She wants me to stamp! She wants to see what will happen, O Suleiman-bin Daoud! You know I can't do it, and now she'll never believe a word I say. She'll laugh at me to the end of my days!'

'No, little brother,' said Suleiman-bin-Daoud, 'she will never laugh at you again,' and he turned the ring on his finger—just for the little Butterfly's sake, not for the sake of showing off,—and, lo and behold, four huge Djinns came out of the earth!

'Slaves,' said Suleiman-bin-Daoud, 'when this gentleman on my finger' (that was where the impudent Butterfly was sitting) 'stamps his left front forefoot you will make my Palace and these gardens disappear in a clap of thunder. When he stamps again you will bring them back carefully.'

'Now, little brother,' he said, 'go back to your wife and stamp all you've a mind to.'

Away flew the Butterfly to his wife, who was crying, 'I dare you to do it! I dare you to do it! Stamp! Stamp now! Stamp!' Balkis saw the four vast Djinns stoop down to the four corners of the gardens with the Palace in the middle, and she clapped her hands softly and said, 'At last Suleiman-bin-Daoud will do for the sake of a Butterfly what he ought to have done long ago for his own sake, and the quarrelsome Queens will be frightened!'

Then the Butterfly stamped. The Djinns jerked the Palace and the gardens a thousand miles into the air: there was a most awful thunder-clap, and everything grew inky-black. The Butterfly's Wife fluttered about in the dark, crying, 'Oh, I'll be good! I'm so sorry I spoke. Only bring the gardens back, my dear darling husband, and I'll never contradict again.'

The Butterfly was nearly as frightened as his wife, and Suleiman-bin-Daoud laughed so much that it was several minutes before he found breath enough to whisper to the Butterfly, 'Stamp again, little brother. Give me back my Palace, most great magician.'

'Yes, give him back his Palace,' said the Butterfly's Wife, still flying about in the dark like a moth. 'Give him back his Palace, and don't let's have any more horrid magic.'

'Well, my dear,' said the Butterfly as bravely as he could, 'you see what your nagging has led to. Of course it doesn't make any difference to *me*—I'm used to this kind of thing—but as a favour to you and to Suleiman-bin-Daoud I don't mind putting things right.'

So he stamped once more, and that instant the Djinns let down the Palace and the gardens, without even a bump. The sun shown on the dark-green orange leaves; the fountains played among the pink Egyptian lilies; the birds went on singing, and the Butterfly's Wife lay on her side under the camphor-tree waggling her wings and panting, 'Oh, I'll be good! I'll be good!'

Suleiman-bin-Daoud could hardly speak for laughing. He leaned back all weak and hiccoughy, and shook his finger at the Butterfly and said, 'O great wizard, what is the sense of returning to me my Palace if at the same time you slay me with mirth!'

Then came a terrible noise, for all the nine hundred and ninety-nine Queens ran out of the Palace shrieking and shouting and calling for their babies. They hurried down the great marble steps below the fountain, one hundred abreast, and the Most Wise Balkis went statelily forward to meet them and said, 'What is your trouble, O Queens?'

They stood on the marble steps one hundred abreast and shouted, '*What* is our trouble?

We were living peacefully in our golden palace, as is our custom, when upon a sudden the Palace disappeared, and we were left sitting in a thick and noisome darkness; and it thundered, and Djinns and Afrits moved about in the darkness! *That* is our trouble, O Head Queen, and we are most extremely troubled on account of that trouble, for it was a troublesome trouble, unlike any trouble we have known.'

Then Balkis the Most Beautiful Queen—Suleiman-bin-Daoud's Very Best Beloved—Queen that was of Sheba and Sabie and the Rivers of the Gold of the South—from the Desert of Zinn to the Towers of Zimbabwe—Balkis, almost as wise as the Most Wise Suleiman-bin-Daoud himself, said, 'It is nothing, O Queens! A Butterfly has made complaint against his wife because she quarrelled with him, and it has pleased our Lord Suleiman-bin-Daoud to teach her a lesson in low-speaking and humbleness, for that is counted a virtue among the wives of the butterflies.'

Then up and spoke an Egyptian Queen—the daughter of a Pharoah—and she said, 'Our Palace cannot be plucked up by the roots like a leek for the sake of a little insect. No! Suleiman-bin-Daoud must be dead, and what we heard and saw was the earth thundering and darkening at the news.'

Then Balkis beckoned that bold Queen

83

without looking at her, and said to her and to the others, 'Come and see.'

They came down the marble steps, one hundred abreast, and beneath his camphor-tree, still weak with laughing, they saw the Most Wise King Suleiman-bin-Daoud rocking back and forth with a Butterfly on either hand, and they heard him say, 'O wife of my brother in the air, remember after this, to please your husband in all things, lest he be provoked to stamp his foot yet again; for he has said that he is used to this magic, and he is most eminently a great magician—one who steals away the very Palace of Suleiman-bin-Daoud himself. Go in peace, little folk!' And he kissed them on the wings, and they flew away.

Then all the Queens except Balkis—the Most Beautiful and Splendid Balkis, who stood apart smiling—fell flat on their faces, for they said, 'If these things are done when a Butterfly is displeased with his wife, what shall be done to us who have vexed our King with our loud-speaking and open quarrelling through many days?'

Then they put their veils over their heads, and they put their hands over their mouths, and they tiptoed back to the Palace most mousy-quiet.

Then Balkis—The Most Beautiful and Excellent Balkis—went forward through the red lilies into the shade of the camphor-tree and laid her hand upon Suleiman-bin-Daoud's shoulder and said, 'O my Lord and Treasure of my Soul, rejoice, for we have taught the Queens of Egypt and Ethiopia and Abyssinia and Persia and India and China with a great and a memorable teaching.'

And Suleiman-bin-Daoud, still looking after the Butterflies where they played in the sunlight, said, 'O my Lady and Jewel of my Felicity, when did this happen? For I have been jesting with a Butterfly ever since I came into the garden.' And he told Balkis what he had done.

Balkis—The tender and Most Lovely Balkis—said, 'O my Lord and Regent of my Existence, I hid behind the camphor-tree and saw it all. It was I who told the Butterfly's Wife to ask the Butterfly to stamp, because I hoped that for the sake of the jest my Lord would make some great magic and that the Queens would see it and be frightened.' And she told him what the Queens had said and seen and thought.

Then Suleiman-bin-Daoud rose up from his seat under the camphor-tree, and stretched his arms and rejoiced and said, 'O my Lady and Sweetener of my Days, know that if I had made a magic against my Queens for the sake of pride or anger, as I made that feast for all the animals, I should certainly have been put to shame. But by means of your wisdom I made the magic for the sake of a jest and for the sake of a little Butterfly, and—behold—it has also delivered me from the vexations of my vexatious wives! Tell me, therefore, O my Lady and Heart of my Heart, how did you come to be so wise?'

And Balkis the Queen, beautiful and tall, looked up into Suleiman-bin-Daoud's eyes and put her head a little on one side, just like the Butterfly, and said, 'First, O my Lord, because I love you; and secondly, O my Lord, because I know what women-folk are.'

Then they went up to the Palace and lived happily ever afterwards.

But wasn't it clever of Balkis?